KASHMIRI COOKING

KRISHNA PRASAD DAR

with

an Introduction and Illustrations

by

CW00688304

PENGUIN BOOKS

Penguin Books India (P) Ltd, 11 Community Centre, Panchsheel Park, New Delhi-110017, India
Penguin Books Ltd., 27 Wrights Lane, London W8 5TZ, UK
Penguin Putnam Inc., 375 Hudson Street, New York, NY 10014, USA
Penguin Books Australia Ltd., Ringwood, Victoria, Australia
Penguin Books Canada Ltd., 10 Alcorn Avenue, Suite 300, Toronto, Ontario M4V 3B2. Canada
Penguin Books (NZ) Ltd., 182-190 Wairau Road, Auckland 10, New Zealand

First published as a BELL Book by Vikas Publishing House (P) Ltd. 1977
First published by Penguin Books India (P) Ltd. 1995

Copyright © Sudhir Dar 1995

10 9 8 7 6 5 4 3

Typeset in Avant Garde by FOLIO, New Delhi-1

*This book is dedicated to
my wife, my children,
grandchildren and
great-grandchildren
and
to
all
lovers
of
good food*

ACKNOWLEDGEMENTS . . .

My warmest thanks to all my near and dear ones who provided invaluable assistance in making this book possible.

To my wife Daya, a devoted companion and my 'severest critic'—in the best sense of the word—I owe many debts. Her sincere, honest criticism over the years has urged me to 'try and try again' to attain perfection.

To Ashok and Sudhir, my sons, who persuaded me to embark on a project so close to my heart. Sudhir has enlivened the book with his illustrations.

To my elder daughter-in-law Rati, who did commendable work in revising and editing the entire text and offering valuable suggestions along the way.

To my younger daughter-in-law Rummy, for taking great pains in scrutinizing and correcting the typescript and the final proofs.

To my grand-daughters Gita, Suniti and Anita, who spent many hours of their spare time taking dictation over several months.

Allahabad, 1977   KRISHNA PRASAD DAR

ACKNOWLEDGMENTS

. . . AND FURTHER ACKNOWLEDGEMENTS

Apart from the three generations of our family who were emotionally involved in the birth of this book, I would like to express my deep sense of gratitude to the following:

Mr Mir Nasrullah, who gladly shared his expert knowledge of Kashmiri Muslim cuisine and revealed some of the traditional recipes which have been a part of the family treasure for generations; the Welcomgroup of Hotels, especially Manjit Gill, a great gourmet chef himself, who personally supervised the preparation of some of the choicest Kashmiri Pandit dishes; Rohit Khattar and Sandeep Tandon of Chor Bizarre fame (and their waza) who produced a royal feast of Kashmiri Muslim food; and Pradeep Dasgupta and his wife Indrani for the superb colour photographs for the front and back covers and their professional touch in creating a visual setting to match the richness of each cuisine.

New Delhi, 1995   SUDHIR DAR

CONTENTS

INTRODUCTION

My father was a gourmet of gourmets, having acquired
the traditional art of Kashmiri Pandit cooking from his
mother and the professional cooks employed
in their home
during his years
of adolescence
and youth. But for
several decades
the   recipes
r e m a i n e d
closetted in his
mind until he
was persuaded
by family and
friends to reveal
the magic of
the   age-old
culinary skills of
one   of   the
world's   finest
cuisines.

Those were the days.

In the early years of this century, every other Kashmiri
Pandit home in the plains had a professional Kashmiri
cook in residence, whose mastery of his art was
demonstrated twice a day, at lunch and dinner. Cooks
came for as little as Rs 10 per month, with food, shelter
and clothing. Pure ghee, then, was less than a rupee a
seer, mustard oil—four seers for a rupee, so one can

imagine the extravagance. Each meal was an event, each dish a gourmet's delight, every day a royal feast.

Over the years, the ladies of the household acquired specialized training from these culinary masters and in due course, became as proficient as their gurus. In another generation, living costs multiplied and less and less homes could bear the heavy expenses of a princely diet. The era of the super cooks was over. Many drifted into government service, others set up mini-restaurants, some became hotel cooks, several returned to Kashmir. Their sons seldom took to the profession. Today, they can be counted on the fingers of one hand. However, they are still available, still as masterly as ever, still the backbone of many a Kashmiri Pandit wedding. Kashmiri Pandit cuisine evolved in the Valley several centuries ago and in course of time absorbed some of the delectable elements of the Mughal art of cooking and, thus enriched, acquired a distinct personality of its own. Hence you will find in this book certain non-vegetarian dishes of Mughal origin which have been given a Kashmiri touch.

Kashmiri cooking developed through the ages as two great schools of culinary craftsmanship—Kashmiri 'Pandit' and 'Muslim'. The basic difference between the two was that the Hindus used 'hing and curd' and the Muslims 'onions and garlic'

Now a few points of interest about the two cuisines.

Though Brahmins, Kashmiri Pandits have generally been great meat eaters. They prefer goat, and preferably, young goat. Meat is usually cut into somewhat large pieces and is mostly chosen from the legs, neck, breast, ribs and shoulder. Curd plays an important part in our cuisine. No meat delicacy, except certain kababs, is cooked without curd. Even in vegetarian dishes, it is often added. Ideally, Kashmiri Pandit food needs heat on two sides (top and bottom) and the best results are obtained from a charcoal fire. However, in these days of electric stoves, gas and pressure cooking, less and less homes use charcoal (an oven serves as a good substitute).

Originally, onions and garlic were never used in Kashmiri Pandit cooking. But as many of us have acquired a taste for them, they have been included in certain recipes as optionals. Though the basic principles of cooking are largely similar in almost all our homes, certain Pandit families have adopted minor changes in both ingredients and methods. The methods given in this book are the ones our family has followed over decades. The book may not be the last word on Kashmiri cooking, but I can assure readers that if the instructions are carefully followed, the results should be satisfying. My father had cooked each dish in this book time and time again, some literally hundreds of times. He was really a master craftsman. Our home in Allahabad was so full of delicious aromas from the kitchen that I couldn't help being hungry all the time I must confess at this point, however, that my own knowledge of Kashmiri food is confined more or less to the fine art of eating! When you've tried your hand with dishes like Kabargah, Kofta, Dum Alu, Methi Chaman, Firni etc., you'll see why.

Kashmiri Muslim cuisine is another gold mine of gourmet cooking to explore, another treasure trove of exotica to savour. Except for some hotels and a few restaurants in India which promote or cater to regional tastes, this highly prized art too has remained largely confined to Kashmiri homes in and out of the Valley. However, professional cooks in Kashmir still continue to thrive, though more and more are beginning to face an uncertain future as the days of lavish hospitality are on the decline and current conditions have reduced the occasions for feasting to traditional festivals, banquets and marriages.

Known as wazas, these cooks are descendants of the master chefs who migrated from Samarkand and parts of Central Asia at the beginning of the fifteenth century and formed a vital part of the entourage that came to Kashmir during the reign of Timur (or Tamarlane). There were 1700 masters of one kind or another. Amongst them were great craftsmen, wood carvers, carpenters, architects, carpet weavers, shawl makers, calligraphists, masters of embroidery and other skilled hands. In the turbulent history of Kashmir, it is considered as an age of renaissance.

As in days of old, the traditional Kashmiri Muslim banquet known as Wazwan is a feast fit for kings. The word 'waz' means chef, a master of culinary arts and 'wan' means the shop with its full array of meats and delicacies. Perhaps nowhere else in India will you find a royal meal as unique and as elaborate as a Wazwan.

It consists of thirty-six courses, of which fifteen to thirty dishes are varieties of meat. Many of the delicacies are cooked through the night under the expert supervision of a 'Vasta Waza' or head chef, assisted by a retinue of wazas. This is Kashmir's most formal meal. It is said that 'the host must lay out all the food he has at his home before his guest and the guest, in turn, must reciprocate the gesture by doing full justice to the meal.' It is not uncommon for a single Kashmiri guest to consume a kilo of meat and perhaps a full chicken at one sitting. But one is expected to savour a little of this and that of the great variety of dishes as they arrive and not indulge in gluttony. However, as lovers of good food some guests find that the urge is irresistible.

The Wazwan is not only a ritual, but a ceremony. Guests are seated in groups of four on a dastarkhan—the traditional cushioned-seating on the floor—and share the meal on a large metal plate called a trami. A 'Tasht-Nari' or wash basin is taken around by attendants so that the guests can wash their hands. The only way to eat is with your fingers. The trami arrives heaped with rice and the first few courses. A typical trami consists of a mound of rice divided by four seekh kababs, four pieces of methi korma, one tabak maaz and two pieces of trami murgh—one safed, one zafrani. Curd and chutney are served in small earthen pots. (If you're ever invited to a Wazwan, remember one simple rule. After each morsel of meat you eat, take a spoonful or two of curd. It helps to digest the richness of the meal).

There are seven standard dishes that are a must for all Wazwans: Rista, Roghan Josh, Tabak Maaz, Daniwal Korma, Aab Gosh, Marchwangan Korma and Gushtaba. Gushtaba is the final dish, the 'full-stop'. It is only after the last trami has been served and the host says 'Bismillah' that the copper covers are lifted and the feast begins.

This book has been a labour of love. My father began to write it when he was eighty and though it took over a year to complete, his great passion for cooking and his lifelong belief that 'if a job is worth doing, it's worth doing well' kept him in good spirits till this mega task was over. In the last stages it became a great family effort and three generations were deeply involved in what we believed was somewhat of a pioneering exercise.

Now the magic formulae are yours.

The book is divided into seven parts. The methods are precise and simple to work on. Savour a little of this, a little of that, but when you settle down to eat, please do justice to the cuisine—eat with your fingers.

SUDHIR DAR

October, 1995

USEFUL INFORMATION

Necessary articles for your kitchen

The number of utensils and gadgets required in any home depends on the size of the family. Many young housewives, especially those who are just beginning to set up a home will find the following list of essential articles for the kitchen a convenient guide.

For everyday Kashmiri cooking it is preferable to have one or two heavy-bottomed brass vessels (degchis/bhagonas) as certain varieties of meat dishes cook best in them. These vessels should be tinned frequently.

Bhagona, with lid (heavy-bottomed)
Chakla (rolling board), with belan (rolling pin)
Chumta (tongs)
Colander (for washing vegetables)
Containers for salt and masalas
Corkscrew
Degchi, with lid (heavy-bottomed)
Dusters
Frying pan
Grater
Grinding stone, with pestle (most homes have a
     mixi these days)
Karchi (ladle)
Karhai (round-bottomed, iron or brass vessel which
     has been tinned inside)
Katoris (small metal bowls)
Kettle
Knives

Pair of scales or a spring scale, with weights
Perforated ladle (jharna)
Sieve
Spoons of different sizes
Strainers
Tava (iron plate, griddle)
Thalis (flat metal plates with low, upturned rims)·
Tin opener
Wooden spoons

And any of the following:
Angeethi (charcoal stove)
Electric stove
Kerosene stove
Gas stove

Weights and measures

500 gm butter	approximately	2 cups
500 gm breadcrumbs	..	4 cups
500 gm dal	..	2 cups
500 gm flour	..	4 cups
500 gm ghee/oil	..	2 cups
500 gm rice	..	2 cups
500 gm rice flour	..	4 cups
500 gm sugar	..	2 cups
50 gm curd	approximately	4 tblsp
125 gm curd	..	$1/2$ cup
100 gm khoya	..	$3/4$ cup
100 gm milk	..	$1/3$ cup
15 gm badam/kaju (shelled)		25 to 30 pieces
15 gm pista (shelled)		55 to 60 pieces
50 gm kishmish	approximately	$1/2$ cup
15 gm dalchini	..	20 sticks
50 gm javitri	..	$3/4$ cup

60 drops	1 teaspoon
2 teaspoons	1 dessertspoon
4 teaspoons	1 tablespoon
2 tablespoons	1 oz
12 tablespoons	1 cup
1 teacup	4 to 5 oz
2 cups	1 pint
4 cups	1 quart
1 tumbler	6 oz
1 pint	1 lb
1 litre	approximately 5 cups
$\frac{1}{2}$ litre	.. $2\frac{1}{2}$ cups
1 handi spoon	.. $3\frac{1}{2}$ tblsps

Oven temperatures

Oven	Temperatures	Regulation setting
Slow	200-250°F	1
Moderate	250-350°F	2
Moderately hot	350-400°F	3 to 5
Hot	400-425°F	6
Very hot	425-450°F	7
Hottest	450-500°F	8 to 9

Different cooking processes

Baking: Cooking by dry heat in an oven or on a hot surface (not by direct exposure to fire).

Bhuno: Browning the meat by adding water and scraping the sediments. Should be continued till the meat gets reddish brown.

Boiling: Softening food in boiling water.

Dum: Cooking by placing live coals on the lid and also under the vessel to soften meat, vegetables, pulao, etc. Can also be done in an oven.

Frying: Cooking in hot ghee, oil or any other fat. Deep frying is done in a large quantity of ghee or oil, in a deep vessel.

Pressure cooking: Cooking under high pressure at a high temperature, in a pressure cooker.

Roasting: Cooking (especially meat) by exposure to open fire. Seekh kababs are an example. Roasting may also be done in an oven (or a tandoor).

Simmering: Cooking on a slow fire over a long period.

Spluttering: Heating/smoking the ghee/oil and putting in the dry, whole spices so that they crackle and release their characteristic aroma.

Steaming: Using double vessels, the outer vessel containing boiling water.

Essential points for good cooking

Be accurate and precise in weights and measures.

Follow recipes carefully.

Do not use more spices than necessary.

Be sure to have good, useful kitchen gadgets to work with.

Look after your utensils and kitchen equipment. Keep them clean.

Get your things together before you begin to cook. It saves time and fuel.

Try new recipes. Make an alteration in the method to suit your taste.

Pour some water on the lid of the vessel to soften the food in it.

Do not use a spoon or ladle when cooking such vegetables as okra or cauliflower, as they tend to break and become pulpy. Instead, hold the vessel with your hands and shake it a few times.

How to economize on food

Do not use more oil or ghee than is necessary. Moreover, it is harmful to health.

Mix a costly vegetable with a cheaper one. You will get a new dish at a lower cost.

Do not peel all vegetables. Peels contain vitamins. Not peeling them also saves time.

Plan your menu in advance so that work can be done quickly and an entire meal be cooked together in a cooker or oven. It saves time, saves fuel.

Do not throw away bones from meat. They make excellent yakhni (stock). Keep in freezer till required.

Try and make snacks and refreshments. Murabbas, jams, sweets of various kinds and namkeen (salted snacks) can be made economically at home.

Dried vegetables

Variety, they say, is the spice of life. Give your family or guests an occasional surprise with a delightful winter vegetable in summer or a sizzling summer dish in winter.

Each year, when certain vegetables are in season and in abundant supply, they may be dried and dehydrated for use during the season when fresh vegetables are scarce. When needed, dried vegetables must first be soaked in water for a few hours, or overnight. They must then be strained, boiled and cooked as prescribed. These have a unique taste of their own, quite different from the packaged, dehydrated vegetables available in the market these days.

Some common vegetables like turnips, cauliflowers, cabbages, tomatoes, radish, beans, peas, etc. are dehydrated as follows:

Turnips (Shaljam)

Take good, large, fresh turnips, peel and cut into fours. Make slices (about three-eights of an inch thick) and spread them out on a cloth in the sun. When bone dry, store in airtight jars or containers. Very small turnips are also dried by dividing the ends in fours with their tender leaves.

Knol-Khol (Ganth Gobhi)
Same as above.

Cauliflower (Phool Gobhi)

Remove the outer leaves. Break the flower into florets. Spread on a cloth. When completely dry, store as above or thread like a garland and dry by hanging them on a peg. Dry in the sun.

Cabbage (Karamkalla)

Take the well-matured, white-leaved variety. Cut into large pieces, say about 10 cm each. Dry as above and store.

Tomatoes (Tamatar)

Clean, slice and spread out on a cloth in the sun. When dry, grind them to a powder, sprinkle a little salt and store in jars. When you use them in a recipe, add lemon juice as dried tomatoes lose their sourness.

Radish (Muli)

Same as cauliflower.

Beans (Sem)

Clean and cut into 1 cm size. Dry as above and store.

Fenugreek (Methi)

Clean all the weeds, wash and spread on a cloth in the sun. When dry, rub lightly with the palms to remove twigs. Store as above. You may mix soya too with methi. Soya can also be dried separately and stored.

Peas (Matar)

Dry them in their shells, in the shade. This preserves the green colour. When dry, shell and store as above.

Spinach (Palak)

Cut off the hard stems and dry.

Combinations of vegetables

Now and again, every cook is in a quandary—what should be cooked? The stock of vegetables may be exactly the same as it was last week or the week before, and one may have run out of interesting menus. Catering to the varied tastes of the family is no easy matter. So how does the poor cook produce something new, different, attractive and palatable every day? Here's how.

Try these simple combinations of vegetables (some of them with meat) and give your family a delicious surprise.

Alu

Dum Alu
Boiled (Rasdaar)
Boiled, with Curd
  (Mattha)
Bharta
Bhujia
With Brinjal
With Okra
With Pumpkin
Khatte
With Bottle Gourd
With Peas
With Fenugreek and
  Soya
With Gherkins
With Onions
With Saag
With Snake Gourd
With Tomatoes
As Kababs

Arvi

Dum
Bhujia
Boiled, with Kalonji and
  Ajwain
Boiled, with Mattha
  and Ajwain
As Kababs
Khatti
With Radish
Rasdaar

Arvi ke Patte

Pakori (Besan)
Khatti
With Curd
With Peethi (Dal)

Baigan

With Potatoes
Bharta
Bhar Ke
Bhujia
With Curd
With Dal (Chana)
With Goli (Meat)
With Radish
Masaledaar
Pakori
Raita
Rasdaar
Tal Ke
With Tomatoes

Banda

Dum
Kabab
Khatta
With Fenugreek

Bhindi

Dum
With Potatoes
Bhujia
With Curd
Khatti
Kurkuri
Raita
Tali
With Tomatoes

Boda/Chowla/Lobhia

With Potatoes
With Yam
Bhujia
With Curd

With Kheema
Khatta
Rasdaar
With Tomatoes

Chukandar

Bhujia
With Tomatoes
Salad

Gajar

Halwa
With Bottle Gourd
Salad
With Tomatoes

Ganth Gobhi

Bhujia
With Curd
Dum
Khatti
With Meat

Hara Dhania/Pudina

Chutney
With any vegetable
As vegetable (Hara
    Dhania only)

Hiksa/Ban Karela

With Potatoes
Bhujia
Khatta
Kurkuri

Kachnal

With Potatoes
Bhujia
With Curd

Khatta
Pakori

Kaddu

With Potatoes
With Chana (Dal)
With Curd
Dum
Bhujia
With Goli (Meat)
With other meat
With Fenugreek
With Radish
Raita
Rasdaar

Kakri

Same as for Kheera

Karam Haak

With Potatoes
With Brinjal
With Chaman (Paneer)

Karamkalla/Bandh Gobhi

With Potatoes
Dum
With Goli (Meat)
With other meat
With Rice
Salad
With Tomatoes

Karela

With Besan
Bhar Ke
Bhujia (with or without
    Potatoes)

With Curd
Dum (with Potatoes)
Meethe Karele
Khatte
Kurkuri

Kathal

With Potatoes
Dum
With Goli
Kabab
Khatta

Kela

With Potatoes
Bhujia
With Curd
Dahi Bara
Kabab

Kheera

With Potatoes
With Curd
Raita
Salad

Kundru

With Potatoes
Bhujia
With Curd
Rasdaar

Lauki

With Potatoes
Bhujia
With Dal
With Curd
Dum
With Meat

With Fenugreek
With Mongochi
Raita
Rasdaar
With Tomatoes

Matar

With Potatoes
With Chaman
Dum
With Cauliflower
With Kheema
With Khoya
With Spinach
With Rice
With Salad
With Tomatoes

Methi

With Chaman
With almost any
    vegetable
With Meat

Muli

With Potatoes
With Potatoes (Khatti)
With Arvi
Bhujia
With Dal (Moong)
With Adrak, Kishmish,
    Nimbu
With Goli (Khatti)
With Pumpkin
Khatti
Pahrathi
Raita
With Snake Gourd

Nadru
With Potatoes
With Curd
Dum
Khatta
With Koftas or Goli

Papita
With Curd
Like Pumpkin
With Lemon Juice
With Mustard Water
    (Achaar)
Salad (Raw)

Parwal
With Potatoes
Bhujia
Bhar Ke
With Curd
Dum
Rasdaar

Patua
With Potatoes
With Brinjal
Chutney
With Beans

Phool Gobhi
With Potatoes
With Curd
With Dal
Dum
With Peas
With Meat
Pakori
With Rice

Salad
With Tomatoes

Pyaz
With Potatoes
Bhujia
Lachcha
Pakori
Raita
Salad

Ratalu
With Curd
Dum
Kabab
Khatte

Razmah
With Potatoes
Bhujia
With Kheema
Rasdaar
With Tomatoes

Saag
With almost all
    vegetables or by
    itself
With Dals (especially
    Palak and Bathua)
Bathua
Yam Leaves
Chane ka saag
Chaulai
With Curd
Kulfa
Marsa
Fenugreek

Methi Palak
Nari ka Saag
Palak
Poi ka Saag
Punarnava (Pathri)
Sarson ka Saag
Soya Methi
Soya Palak

Sehjan

With Potatoes
Bhujia
With Curd
Rasdaar

Sem

With Potatoes
Bhujia
With Brinjal
With Curd
Khatte
With Tomatoes

Shakarkand

Boiled
With Curd
Khatta
Kheer

Shaljam

Bhujia
In Dal (Arhar)
In Dal (Moong)
Dried
Dum

With Meat
In Mustard Water
    (Pani ka Achaar)

Tinda

With Potatoes
Bhar Ke
Dum
Rasdaar

Tamatar

With any vegetable
Bhar Ke
Chutney
With Dal
With Meat
Raita
With Rice
Salad

Turai

With Potatoes
With Chaman
With Curd
Khatti
With Meat
With Fenugreek
With Radish

Zaminkand

With Curd
Dum
Kabab
Khatta
With Fenugreek

SPICES

GARAM MASALA
(Pungent Spices Powder)

125 gm zeera
15 gm laung
125 gm bari elaichi
125 gm methi dana
10 gm dalchini

125 gm sonf
15 gm choti elaichi
15 tejpattas
5 gm javitri
2 jaiphal

In a karhai or thick-bottomed vessel roast the zeera, laung, elaichi (bari), methi dana and dalchini till they begin to turn reddish brown. Remove from fire. Now pound these and the other ingredients (unroasted) to a fine powder. Sieve, and store the masala in air-tight containers.

Makes : approximately 500 gms of garam masala.

DHANIA
(Coriander Powder)

Dhania seeds should be roasted till light brown and then powdered, and stored in air-tight containers.

HALDI
(Turmeric Powder)

Haldi is pounded and sieved through a fine sieve and stored in powdered form in air-tight containers.

SONTH
(Dried Ginger Powder)

Sonth is pounded and sieved like haldi and stored in powdered form in air-tight containers.

LAL MIRCH
(Red Chilli Powder)

Lal Mirch should be dried in the sun, powdered and stored in air-tight containers.

PETHE KI BARI
(Ash Gourd in Mixed Spice Cakes)

500 gm urad dal (dhuli)	50 gm peppercorns
125 gm petha (pulp)	(crushed coarsely)
$1/_2$ tsp hing (powdered	60 gm raw dhania seeds
and diluted in water)	(crushed)
50 gm lal mirch powder	2 tsp zeera

Wash and soak the dal overnight. Next morning, strain and grind it coarsely. In a bowl mix the ground dal, petha pulp, hing, lal mirch, peppercorns, dhania and zeera and mix well. Keep the dough in a warm place for several hours to allow it to rise and ferment a little, preferably during the night.

Next morning drop a tablespoonful of this mixture, at a time, on an oiled thali, till it is full of small baris. Dry them in the sun for a few days and store in air-tight containers.

SUCCH BARI
(Mixed Spice Cakes)

125 gm methi dana
$^1/_2$ kg dhuli urad dal (atta)
60 gm lal mirch powder
100 gm garam masala
200 gm mustard oil

60 gm dhania powder (roasted)
$^1/_2$ tsp hing (diluted in hot water)

Place a karhai or griddle on fire, add the methi dana, roast till light brown and grind it to a fine powder.

In a bowl, put in the urad atta and mix the methi dana powder and other ingredients, thoroughly. Now add the oil, the diluted hing and rub the oil into the atta for about fifteen minutes so that it is well absorbed by the atta. Now add water, a little at a time and knead it well to form a stiff dough. On kneading, the dough will increase in bulk. Keep it in a bhagona overnight. The more it ferments, the better the bari.

Next morning, oil a thali, and make small baris of any shape you prefer, and dry them in the sun for a few days, till completely dry. The usual shape of baris is like small discs, two to three inches round and a quarter of an inch thick. A quicker method of shaping baris is to make a thick bread-shaped roll, and cut it into slices a quarter of an inch thick with a sharp knife. Baris may be stored, as they are, in air-tight containers, or crushed to form a powder.

Note : For a better and more economical method of flavouring dishes, powdered laung and hing, in equal parts, are made into a solution with water. Two tablespoons of this mixture are added to the ghee or oil before frying any vegetable or meat dish. This is a better substitute than hing or laung used separately.

KABARGAH
(Batter-fried Mutton Ribs)

10 breast pieces of mutton, with 2 ribs each	$1/_2$ litre milk
	125 gm gram flour
	50 gm rice flour
4 choti elaichis	salt to taste
1 tsp sonf	$1/_2$ tsp lal mirch powder
4 pieces of laung	a pinch of hing
1 inch piece dalchini	125 gm ghee

Tie the elaichi, sonf, laung and dalchini in a piece of cotton cloth and place them, with the meat, milk and half a litre of water in a degchi, on the fire. Boil for thirty minutes or more till the meat becomes tender and the liquid evaporates. While the meat is cooking, prepare a batter of gram and rice flour with a little water. Mix well till it acquires a light consistency. (To test the batter, drop a teaspoon of it into a cup of water. If the batter floats, the consistency is correct; if not, beat again.) Add salt, lal mirch and hing to the batter and mix well. Dip the pieces of boiled meat in the batter and fry till they are golden brown.

Serves : 5

ROGHAN JOSH
(Mutton Curry)

1 kg meat (preferably
  dast or front leg)
300 gm ghee or
  vegetable oil
275 gm curd
salt to taste
4 pieces of laung
a pinch of hing
1 tsp sonth powder
1 tsp lal mirch powder
  (preferably roghni)
1 inch piece dalchini

2 inch piece ginger
  (ground)
1 tsp sugar
2 tsp garam masala
a pinch of zafran
1 tsp keora water
100 gm khoya
25 gm badam (soaked
  and skinned)
approximately 3 cups
  water

Heat the oil/ghee in a heavy-bottomed degchi and add the laung, hing, dalchini, the cut pieces of meat, 250 gm curd, ground ginger, lal mirch and sonth. Cover and allow to simmer on low heat till all the water evaporates and a reddish sediment begins to appear. Stir occasionally to prevent burning. Then put in two tablespoons of water and cover again. After a few moments, scrape the sediment with a spatula, turning the meat all the time.

Repeat this process till the meat turns reddish brown. Then add sugar and the water and cook for at least half an hour. When the meat becomes tender, add the garam masala and zafran (ground to a paste with some keora water) and cover for another ten minutes. When the meat is nearly done, add the khoya (thinned with 25 gm of curd) and badam, ground to a paste. Place the vessel on a slow fire and cook for a few minutes till the khoya turns red and there is a little gravy left.

Serves : 6

QALIA
(Mutton Ribs in thin Turmeric Gravy)

1 kg meat (chops and
    breast, with 2 ribs in
    each)
250 gm ghee or
    vegetable oil
salt to taste
a pinch of hing
200 gm curd
4 pieces of laung
1 tsp lal mirch powder
2 inch piece ginger
    (ground)

1 tsp sonth powder
1 heaped tsp haldi powder
1 tsp sonf
250 gm turnips or
    potatoes (peeled and
    cut in fours)
2 tsp garam masala
1 tsp sugar
a bunch of hara dhania
    leaves (finely chopped)
approximately 3 cups
    water

Heat the ghee/oil in a heavy-bottomed degchi, add the hing, curd, laung, meat, salt, lal mirch, ground ginger and sonth. Cover and allow to simmer on low heat till all the water evaporates and a reddish sediment begins to appear. Stir occasionally to prevent burning. Then put in two tablespoons of water and cover again. After a few moments, scrape the sediment with a spatula, turning the meat all the time. Repeat the process till the meat turns brown. Then add water and cook for at least half an hour. When the meat is well cooked, add the haldi and turn it a few times. Add water and allow to simmer.

Put the sonf in a small muslin bag and place the bag in the vessel with the meat. Add turnips or potatoes. Pour in the water and cook till the meat is tender. Remove the muslin bag. Then add garam masala and sugar, together with hara dhania. (The gravy should be thin, but not watery.)

Serves : 6

QORMA
(Mutton in Creamy Sauce)

The recipe is the same as for Roghan Josh, but in this case the water in the gravy must be allowed to evaporate so that only the fat remains.

SAFED SALAN
(Mutton in Milk Sauce)

1 kg meat (dast and breast pieces)
200 gm ghee or vegetable oil
6 pieces of laung
1 inch piece dalchini
salt to taste

1 tsp lal mirch powder
20 peppercorns
1 tsp sugar
$1/2$ tblsp garam masala
250 ml milk
4-5 cups water

Cut the meat into three-inch pieces and the breast with two ribs attached. Heat the ghee in a degchi and add the laung, dalchini, lal mirch, peppercorns, meat and salt. Keep turning till the meat is light brown. Add sugar and sufficient water. Allow to simmer for half an hour on a medium fire. When the meat is tender, add garam masala and slowly pour in the milk. Cook on a slow fire for another few minutes. The gravy will turn reddish white. Safed Salan tastes best when eaten with chapattis.

Serves : 6

PASANDE
(Flattened Mutton Pieces in Gravy)

1 kg meat (raan or hind leg)	1 tsp sonth powder
300 gm ghee or vegetable oil	2 tsp dhania powder
6 pieces of laung	a pinch of hing
2 medium onions (ground; optional)	2 inch piece ginger (ground)
6 cloves garlic (ground; optional)	a pinch of zafran
150 gm curd	1 tsp keora water
salt to taste	a bunch of hara dhania leaves (finely chopped)
1 tsp lal mirch powder	2 tsp garam masala
	approximately ½ cup water

Trim the meat, and carefully cut it into long, flat pieces, (about two inches wide and four to five inches long). Beat gently with a meat mallet or heavy knife, so that the pieces are scored, though on one side only. These are pasandas.

Heat ghee in a degchi and add laung and the pasandas (and garlic and onions, if used). Cover and cook till the water from the meat has dried. Add curd, salt, sonth, lal mirch, hing and ginger. Cover and cook on low heat till the meat has browned. When a reddish sediment appears, scrape with the spatula and add two tablespoons of water. Repeat this process, stirring occasionally.

Add the water and cook till the meat is tender. Turn the pasandas over gently. Grind the zafran in keora water, and add it to the meat along with the garam masala and dhania. The pasandas should not have much gravy. Garnish with hara dhania when almost ready.

Variation : If desired, fried potatoes, cut in half, may be added to the pasandas at the time of cooking.

Serves : 6

SHABDEGH
(Mughlai Mutton with Turnips)

1 kg lean meat (front leg, breast and chops)	2 inch piece ginger (ground)
salt to taste	$1/2$ kg medium sized turnips (peeled and cut into fours)
1 tblsp sonf	
2 tsp garam masala	
1 tsp lal mirch powder	1 tsp sugar
2 tsp haldi powder	1 bunch hara dhania leaves (finely chopped)
4 pieces of laung	
200 gm curd	5 cups water

Heat ghee in a degchi, add the hing, laung, meat, salt and lal mirch. Fry till reddish brown, adding water to prevent burning. After frying, put the sonf and garam masala in a small muslin bag, place it in the degchi. Add the other masalas, ginger and curd and at least one litre of water. Allow to simmer for two to three hours. When the meat becomes soft and starts sticking to the fingers, add turnips and sugar and cook for another half hour. Cooking should be done on a slow fire for about three to four hours, adding water off and on. As the name Shabdegh implies, cooking commences in the evening and lasts almost till midnight. When ready there should be a little gravy left. Remove the muslin bag. Garnish with hara dhania.

Serves : 6

CHOPS

1 kg chops (with 2 ribs each)	salt and lal mirch powder to taste
2 medium onions	1 tblsp vinegar
6 cloves garlic	125 gm ghee or vegetable oil
2 inch piece ginger	white of an egg
2 inch piece papaya	breadcrumbs
¹/₂ inch piece dalchini	1 big onion (shredded, for garnish)
6 peppercorns	
2 tsp garam masala	
50 gm curd	

Remove a rib from each chop and trim. Flatten the chops, using the blunt edge of a knife. Grind to a fine paste the onions, garlic, ginger, papaya, dalchini and peppercorns. Then add garam masala, salt, lal mirch, vinegar and curd. Smear the chops with this paste, on both sides, and set aside for an hour.

Drain the vinegar from the chops, dip each piece in the lightly-beaten egg-white, and coat with breadcrumbs. Put two tablespoons of ghee on a tava or in a frying pan, and shallow fry till golden brown. Serve with tomato sauce and shredded onions.

Serves : 6

DUM RAAN
(Spiced Mutton Baked with Curd and Papaya)

1 kg meat (raan or hind leg)	3 medium onions
salt to taste	2 inch piece raw papaya
250 gm curd	$1/2$ tblsp garam masala
juice of one lemon	250 gm ghee or vegetable oil
6 cloves garlic	1 tsp lal mirch powder
2 inch piece ginger	1 tsp sonth powder
a pinch of hing	100 gm khoya
8 peppercorns	1 tsp sugar

Trim the raan and smear it with salt, curd and lemon juice and set aside for fifteen minutes. Grind together the garlic, ginger, hing, peppercorns, onions and papaya to a smooth paste. Rub this over the meat and prick it deeply all over with a fork. Smear with garam masala, and let it stand for two hours.

Heat the ghee in a heavy-bottomed degchi and place it on a slow fire. Take a piece of muslin and place the raan, lal mirch, sonth, khoya and sugar in it. Tie the muslin and put it in the degchi, with one cup of water. (If a pressure cooker is used, two cups of water are required.) Keep turning the raan over, so that it is cooked on both sides. (This is not necessary, if pressure-cooked.) When the meat is quite tender and the gravy has almost dried, take the raan out carefully, place on a serving dish, and squeeze the masala from the muslin over it.

Serves : 6

KOFTA
(Minced Meat Rolls in Gravy)

1 kg mince (made from
the raan or hind leg)
salt to taste
1 tsp lal mirch powder
1 tsp sonth powder
2 tsp dhania powder
2 tsp zeera powder
2 tsp garam masala
2 inch piece ginger
(ground)
4 pieces of laung

a bunch of hara dhania
leaves (finely chopped)
a pinch of hing
250 gm curd
2 tblsp mustard oil
100 gm khoya
300 gm ghee or
vegetable oil
a pinch of zafran (ground
in 1 tsp keora water)
2 cups water

Mix well the lal mirch, sonth, dhania, zeera, garam masala, salt, ginger, hara dhania and two-thirds of the curd into the mince. Then blend the mustard oil with the meat, knead well and set aside for about one hour. Add khoya and knead again.

In a wide-mouthed degchi, put in the ghee, the remaining curd, half a cup of water, laung and hing. While this simmers, roll the meat by hand, making each piece about three to four inches long and three-quarters of an inch thick. (The meat may be rolled by hand over a flat metal plate.) Slip each piece carefully into the vessel, shaking the container from time to time to

prevent the koftas from sticking to the bottom. This step is necessary as the meat will release some water. As it dries and the koftas begin to stick, add two to three tablespoons of water to the koftas and cover the vessel. Wait for a few minutes, then uncover and shake the vessel, in a circular motion, so as to separate the koftas from each other. Carefully scrape the sediment from the vessel with a spatula. Repeat till the koftas are quite brown. Add the water and cover again. Cook for twenty minutes. When the gravy thickens, remove the vessel from the fire, and add the zafran ground in keora water.

Makes : approximately 35 koftas

Serves : 8-10

GOLI METHI
(Meat Balls with Fenugreek)

The ingredients are the same as for Kofta. Instead of khoya, use the following additions:

50 gm fresh fenugreek   1 cup water
(ground to a paste) or   1 heaped tsp haldi powder
2 tblsp dried fenugreek

Prepare as for Kofta, except that the meat should be rolled into little balls, not larger than marbles. Fry the golis till they turn reddish brown and then add the fenugreek. Fry both together on a slow fire till the fenugreek darkens and releases its aroma, adding a tablespoon of water to prevent the golis from sticking to the bottom of the pan. Now add the haldi and water, and allow to simmer for about twenty minutes till the gravy thickens. Be careful not to overfry the fenugreek as it is likely to burn and turn bitter. Add keora or zafran if desired.

Makes : 40-45 golis

Serves : 8-10

SHUFTA
(Minced Meat with Peas)

1 kg mince (raan or hind leg, coarsely ground)
300 gm ghee or vegetable oil
250 gm curd
salt to taste
4 pieces of laung
1 tsp sonth powder
a pinch of hing
1 tsp lal mirch powder
2 inch piece ginger (ground)

500 gm peas (shelled)
250 gm hara dhania leaves (finely chopped)
1 tsp keora water
a pinch of zafran (ground to a paste)
1 tsp sugar
2 tsp garam masala
1 tsp dhania powder
100 gm khoya
approximately 1 1/2 cups water

Heat the ghee in a degchi. Add the hing, laung, meat, curd, sonth, lal mirch, ginger and salt. Stir and add water occasionally to prevent burning. Cook well till the meat turns reddish brown. Add sugar, peas and turn it a few times. Pour in the water and allow the meat to simmer for about twenty minutes. When a little gravy is left, add hara dhania, keora water, zafran, garam masala and dhania. Next, put in the khoya (diluted with the remaining curd) and cook till it turns light brown. Place the vessel on a slow fire, cover and put a few live charcoals on the lid, for a few minutes. Cook till the gravy thickens, then remove.

Serves : 8

DOPYAZA
(Spiced Mutton Mince)

1 kg meat (raan or hind leg, coarsely ground)	1 tsp lal mirch powder
300 gm ghee or mustard oil	2 inch piece ginger (ground)
250 gm curd	1 tsp haldi powder
salt to taste	4 tsp amchur powder
4 pieces of laung	1 tsp dhania powder
1 tsp sonth powder	2 tsp garam masala
a pinch of hing	500 gm hara dhania leaves (finely chopped)

Heat the ghee/oil in a tinned degchi, add the laung, sonth, hing, ginger, meat, curd, lal mirch, haldi and water. Fry for thirty minutes, constantly adding a tablespoon or two of water to prevent burning. When the meat becomes tender and a little gravy is left, add the amchur, dhania, garam masala and hara dhania. Cook for another ten minutes on a slow fire, remove and serve.

Variations : Freshly-cut pudina or hara dhania and peas can be used instead of just hara dhania.

Note : For 1 kg of meat use 500 gm of hara dhania or shelled peas.

Serves : 8

GOLI KHATTI
(Sour Meat Balls)

The ingredients are the same as for Kofta except for khoya and fenugreek. Instead, add:

2 tblsp amchur or ¹/₂ cup lemon juice   **1 heaped tsp haldi**

Prepare as for Goli Methi. When the golis are almost ready, add the amchur or lemon juice, and allow to simmer till ready. Garnish with hara dhania or pudina.

Variations : Vegetables like radish, cut into rounds—or tomatoes may be added and cooked with the golis, after they have been fried. If tomatoes are used, skin them by pouring boiling water over them or use tomato puree. Do not add amchur; use a teaspoon of sugar instead.

Makes : 40-45 golis

Serves : 8-10

GOLI WITH DAL
(Meat Balls with Lentils)

The ingredients are the same as for Kofta except for khoya. Use instead:

250 gm urad dal (dhuli)   **50 gm ghee, for frying**

Prepare golis in the usual manner. (See recipe for Goli Methi) After they turn reddish brown, add a cup of water and allow to simmer till tender.

In a separate vessel, fry the dal lightly and add enough water to just cover it. Cook till it is half done. Then add the golis and simmer over a slow fire till the gravy dries. Garnish with chopped hara dhania.

Serves : 8-10

SHAMI KABAB
(Minced Meat Kababs)

1 kg mince (raan or hind leg; finely ground)
250 gm chana dal
salt to taste
6 pieces of laung
1 inch stick dalchini
6 choti elaichis
3 bari elaichis
1 tsp zeera
1 tsp lal mirch powder
6 cloves garlic (optional)
8 peppercorns
2 inch piece ginger (ground)
3 medium onions, sliced and fried (optional)
2 tsp dhania powder
50 gm hara dhania leaves (finely chopped)
2 hari mirch (finely chopped)
2 eggs (optional)
1 slice bread, soaked in a little water and crumbled (optional)
juice of one lemon
250 gm ghee or oil for frying
2 tsp garam masala
approximately 4 cups water

Place the finely minced meat in a vessel containing the water, and add all the ingredients up to peppercorns. Boil till the meat turns soft, pulpy and almost dry. Remove from heat. Grind finely the cooked meat in a grinder/food processor. Add garam masala, ginger, fried onions, dhania, hara dhania, hari mirch, eggs and bread. Mix well, and add lemon juice. Form the mixture into flat rounds, half-inch thick and two and a half or three inches in diameter. Heat the ghee, and when really hot, fry the kababs, two or three at a time. Brown well and remove from fire, and place on a sheet of paper so that the excess oil is absorbed.

Makes : 35-40 kababs

Serves : 8

GULAR KABAB
(Minced Meat Kababs with Orange Filling)

1 kg meat (raan or hind leg; finely minced)	1 tsp garam masala
250 gm chana dal	3 inch piece ginger (diced)
5 tblsp arrowroot	50 gm hara dhania leaves (finely chopped)
salt to taste	
2 tsp dhania powder	4 hari mirch (finely chopped)
1 tsp lal mirch powder	
250 gm ghee or oil for frying	1 orange (peeled and segmented, skinned and crumbled)
1 tsp sugar	

Boil the meat and chana dal in four cups of water till it is tender and all the water has evaporated. Grind it finely on a grinding stone. Add two tablespoons arrowroot, salt, dhania, lal mirch and garam masala. Mix well. Also, mix in the hari mirch, hara dhania, ginger, crumbled orange segments and sugar. This forms the filling.

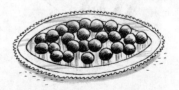

Take small portions of meat in one hand, flattening them with the other. Put half a teaspoon of filling in each, rolling it slowly into a ball, one inch in diameter. Repeat, till all the meat is finished. Then, roll each ball in the remaining arrowroot, and deep fry in a karhai, till light brown.

Makes : 35-40 kababs

Serves : 8

SEEKH KABAB
(Skewered Mince Rolls)

1 kg mince (raan or hind
　　leg)
100 gm roasted gram
2 medium onions sliced
　　(optional)
2 inch piece ginger
6 cloves garlic

1 tsp zeera
2 inch square piece raw
　　papaya
salt and lal mirch
　　powder to taste
2 tsp dhania powder
100 gm ghee

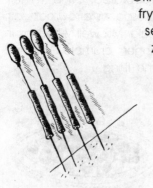

Grind the roasted gram finely, and fry the onions till brown. Grind separately the ginger, garlic, zeera, fried onions and raw papaya. Add these to the meat, together with the salt, lal mirch and dhania, and mix well. Next, take iron rods, a quarter of an inch in diameter, and cover the middle portion with a handful of the prepared meat, holding the rod vertically. Press the meat with the palm of your hand till it is about seven inches long and one inch thick. Dip your hand in water occasionally so that the meat doesn't stick to the hand. Place the rods on supports, three or four inches above a charcoal fire, and rotate gradually so that the seekh is roasted all round. Do not keep the rod too close to the fire. Soak a piece of cloth in ghee and squeeze it over the kababs two or three times while roasting. When they are quite brown, gently slide the kababs off the rod on to a serving dish. Garnish with finely sliced onion rings, and serve immediately.

Variation : Put the roasted kababs into a frying pan with a little ghee, and shallow fry them.

Makes : 30 kababs

Serves : 8

MUTTON CUTLETS

1 kg mince (raan or hind leg; finely ground)
2 tsp dhania powder
2 hari mirch (finely chopped)
salt and lal mirch powder to taste
2 onions (chopped)
a pinch of hing
1 tsp sonth powder
2 pieces of laung
2 inch piece ginger (ground)
a bunch of hara dhania leaves (finely chopped)
2 tsp garam masala
15 medium potatoes
breadcrumbs, rice flour or arrowroot
2 egg whites (beaten)
200 gm ghee or vegetable oil

Cook meat as for Dopyaza, using 50 gm of ghee and all the ingredients, except potatoes and breadcrumbs. Dry the meat.

Boil the potatoes; cool, peel and mash. Mix in a little salt and lal mirch to taste. Form into flat rounds about two inches in diameter, and sandwich the meat between two of these. Press sides down with your thumb and form into rounds or ovals. Repeat, till all the meat and potatoes are used. Roll the cutlets in the egg white and breadcrumbs and deep fry, three or four at a time, till golden brown. Place on a sheet of paper to absorb the excess ghee or oil.

Makes : 30 cutlets

Serves : 8

KHEEMA WITH CHANE KI DAL
(Minced Meat with Yellow Lentils)

The ingredients are the same as for Dopyaza (except for amchur), with the addition of

**250 gm chana dal
(soaked for an hour
and washed)**

**a bunch of hara dhania
leaves (finely chopped)**

Fry as you would Dopyaza. When the meat has almost browned, add the dal and fry for a few minutes more. Then add haldi and two cups of water. Cook on low heat, adding more water if necessary till the dal is tender and dry, and all the water has evaporated. Season with hara dhania.

Serves : 8-10

KABAB SHIKAMPURI
(Kababs with Orange Filling)

The ingredients are the same as for Shami Kabab, except for the filling which is as follows:

a bunch of hara dhania leaves (finely chopped)
1 large orange (peeled and segmented, skinned and crumbled)
10-15 gm kishmish

50 gm ginger (finely diced)
4 hari mirch (finely chopped)
2 onions, finely chopped (optional)

Fill as for Gular Kabab. Flatten, and deep fry.

Makes : 35-40 kababs

Serves : 8

KABAB MALAI
(Kababs in Sweetened Cream)

The ingredients are the same as for Gular Kabab, except for the filling.

This is malai or cream, mixed with a little misri or sugar. The kababs are usually oblong in shape. (Make sure the malai has a thick consistency.)

KABAB NARGISI
(Boiled Eggs covered with Mince)

½ kg mince (raan or hind leg)
12 eggs
2 inch piece ginger (ground)
6 cloves garlic (ground)
salt to taste

1 tsp lal mirch powder
1 tsp dhania powder
2 tsp garam masala
2 medium onions (ground to a paste and fried)
150 gm ghee
arrowroot for coating

Boil ten eggs for eight minutes. Plunge them in cold water and shell. Boil half the meat in water till it is soft and dry. Mix it with the raw meat. Now mix the remaining two (unboiled) eggs in the mixture of boiled eggs and raw meat. Add salt, the spices, fried onions, the garlic and ginger paste. Mix well. Now take one egg at a time and coat it all over with the meat and roll it in a little arrowroot. Deep fry in a karhai till they are medium brown in colour. Before serving, cut kababs into two with a sharp knife.

Serves : Depends on the servings of kababs per person.

PASANDA KABAB
(Pounded Meat Kababs)

1 kg meat (raan or hind leg)
2 inch piece papaya
2 inch piece ginger
6 cloves garlic (optional)
2 medium onions (optional)
100 gm ghee

6 peppercorns
2 hari mirch (finely chopped)
salt and lal mirch powder to taste
a pinch of hing
1 tsp garam masala

Cut the meat into three or four inch slices, half an inch thick, and beat lightly on one side as for pasandas. Grind to a fine paste the papaya, ginger, garlic, onions, peppercorns and hari mirch. Then add salt, lal mirch, hing and garam masala. Smear this mixture on both sides of the pasandas and set aside for an hour. Now roll each pasanda and secure with a string. Pour the ghee into a frying pan and fry them on a slow fire. Cover all the pasandas with a lid, placing some live charcoals on top. Cook till reddish brown.

Serves : 8

GALAVAT KE KABAB
(Soft, Spicy Kababs)

1 kg mince (raan or hind leg)	2 bari elaichis
2 inch piece raw papaya	2 tsp dhania powder
6 peppercorns	4 pieces of laung
salt and lal mirch powder to taste	100 gm roasted chana
	100 gm ghee
	2 onions

Grind papaya, one onion and the peppercorns to make a paste, add salt and lal mirch. Chop the other onion finely and fry. Roast the elaichi, dhania and laung and grind separately, as also the roasted chana. Add all this to the finely minced meat, except half the chana. Knead the meat mixture well and set aside for two hours.

When starting to make the kababs, add the remaining chana and knead well again. On a tava or frying pan, pour two or three teaspoons of ghee and when hot, place small portions of meat on it, pressing them flat with the fingers. Fry till brown on both sides. Add ghee in small quantities as you continue frying. These kababs are usually very soft and must be handled carefully.

Makes : 30-35 kababs

Serves : 8

KACHCHE GOSHT KE KABAB
(Spicy Kababs)

This recipe is almost the same as that for Galavat ke Kabab, except that no papaya is used. The minced meat is mixed with the masala, etc., and formed into flat rounds. They are then shallow fried till reddish brown and later cooked in a frying pan, using a little water. The water should be allowed to evaporate so that the kababs are dry.

Serves : 8

KALEJI KE KABAB
(Liver Kababs)

½ kg liver (trimmed and cut into 1 inch pieces)

50 gm curd

salt and lal mirch powder to taste

2 medium onions (finely chopped and fried)

2 inch piece ginger (ground)

a pinch of hing

2 hari mirch (finely chopped)

1 tsp sonth powder

1 tsp garam masala

1 tsp dhania powder

50 gm hara dhania leaves (finely chopped)

25 gm rice flour

150 gm ghee for frying

Boil the liver in a cup of water. Add the curd and all the ingredients up to sonth. When the liver is tender and dry, grind it to a fine paste on a grinding stone. Now add the garam masala, dhania and hara dhania. Mix in the rice flour, roll into koftas and deep fry till golden brown.

Makes : 15-20 kababs

Serves : 6

MACHHLI KE KABAB
(Fish Kababs)

1 kg fish (tingra or
   singhara)
2 medium onions
2 eggs
salt to taste
1 tsp lal mirch powder

2 tsp dhania powder
1 tsp garam masala
juice of one lemon
1 cup breadcrumbs
200 gm ghee or
   vegetable oil

Boil fish for five minutes, drain and allow to cool. Remove skin and bones, and mash. In a little ghee, fry the onions till light brown, add fish, and stir till the moisture evaporates. Remove from heat and add salt, spices and lemon juice and mix again. Form into balls, then flatten. Coat with breadcrumbs, and deep fry till golden brown.

Makes : 35-40 kababs

Serves : 8

GURDE KAPURE
(Kidneys and Testes Curry)

6 kidneys, 6 testes
(trimmed and cut in
half, lengthwise)
125 gm ghee or
vegetable oil
$1/2$ tsp sonth powder
$1/2$ tsp lal mirch powder.
a pinch of hing
2 pieces of laung
salt to taste

100 gm curd
1 tsp dhania powder
1 tsp garam masala
$1^1/_2$ inch piece ginger
(ground to a paste)
$1/_4$ tsp keora water
a bunch of hara dhania
leaves (finely chopped)
$1^1/_2$ cup water

Put ghee in a tinned degchi and place on a slow fire.
Add the sonth, lal mirch, hing, laung, salt and curd,
and fry till the masala turns red and the water
evaporates. Put in the kidneys and fry till they are light
brown. Then add the testes and fry carefully (they
break easily) till brown. Pour in a cup of water and
simmer for fifteen minutes on a slow fire. Test by hand
to see if the kidneys have softened. Then add dhania,
garam masala, ginger paste, keora and hara dhania. If
the kidneys are still not done, add another half a cup
of water and simmer, making sure that the gravy is fairly
thick.

Serves : 4-6

KALEJI
(Liver Curry)

1 kg liver, and lungs and
    heart (optional)
salt to taste
1 tsp sonth powder
250 gm curd
a pinch of hing
4 pieces of laung
2 cups water
$\frac{1}{2}$ tsp keora water
a pinch of zafran

250 gm ghee or mustard
    oil (kaleji cooks best
    in mustard oil)
2 inch piece ginger
    (ground)
1 tsp lal mirch powder
2 tsp dhania powder
2 tsp garam masala
a bunch of hara dhania
    leaves (finely chopped)

In a tinned degchi, put in the liver (cut into half-inch pieces), salt, sonth, curd, hing, laung and water. Boil till the water evaporates. Then add ghee or oil, ginger and lal mirch and fry till a reddish sediment begins to appear. Then put in two tablespoons of water and cover again. When the liver turns reddish brown and just a little gravy remains, put in the dhania, garam masala, hara dhania, keora and zafran (ground to a paste with a little keora water). Add a cup of water and cook till tender. (Pudina leaves may be substituted for hara dhania). Place the vessel on a slow fire and put a few live charcoals on the lid of the vessel for fifteen minutes. Remove and serve.

Variation : Liver may also be prepared as a sour dish by adding one-third cup of lemon juice or two tablespoons of amchur, when the meat is almost ready.

Serves : 6-8

BHEJA
(Brain Curry)

6 goats' brains (about
  $1/2$ kg)
65 gm ghee or
  vegetable oil
100 gm curd
salt to taste
$1/4$ tsp lal mirch powder
$1/2$ tsp sonth powder
a pinch of hing

2 pieces of laung
$1^1/2$ inch piece ginger
  (ground to a paste)
$1/2$ tsp dhania powder
$1/2$ tsp garam masala
$1/4$ tsp keora water
a bunch of hara dhania
  leaves (finely chopped)

Put the ghee in a tinned degchi and place it on a slow fire. Add curd, salt, lal mirch, sonth, hing and laung and fry till the water evaporates and the masala leaves the sides of the vessel and turns red. Remove and set aside.

Tie the brains in a piece of cloth or muslin bag and place in another vessel containing enough water to cover the brains. Boil for five minutes. When they set and become a little hard, remove from the fire, take out of cloth, and cut into fours or sixes. Place the pieces in the fried masala on a slow fire for ten minutes, till the water almost evaporates. Add ginger paste, dhania, garam masala, keora and hara dhania and simmer for a few more minutes. Remove and serve.

Serves : 4-6

CHUSTE
(Spiced Curry of Goat's Intestines)

3 feet of intestines
100 gm ghee or
    vegetable oil
1 tsp garam masala
1 tsp dhania powder
salt and lal mirch
    powder to taste
1 inch piece ginger
    (ground)
$1/2$ tsp sonth powder

a pinch of hing
2 hari mirch (finely
    chopped)
100 gm curd
$1/2$ tsp sugar
1 cup rice
1 tsp succh bari
    (powdered)
$1/2$ tsp zeera powder
25 gm desi ghee

Cut intestines into three pieces (one foot each) and hold one end at the mouth of a tap. After squeezing them out, clean thoroughly in running water. Now reverse the tubes and clean again. Cut the intestines into pieces, three-quarters of an inch long and boil in salted water for ten minutes, till tender. Drain and set aside.

Heat ghee in a degchi, add all the masalas (except succh bari and zeera), hari mirch, curd and sugar, and fry.

Cook rice in a separate vessel in four cups of water, stirring frequently till it becomes a paste. When reduced to a thick batter, add cooked intestines and succh bari and leave on a low fire. Do not allow it to thicken. Add hot water if required till it attains the consistency of thick dal.

When done, season with zeera fried in desi ghee.

Serves : 2-4

PAYE KI YAKHNI
(Trotters' Soup)

$^1/_2$ kg goats' trotters
    (cleaned and cut into
    2 inch pieces, marrow
    intact)
2 medium onions
    (chopped)
15 gm desi ghee

2 tblsp semolina
6 choti elaichis
2 pieces of laung
$^1/_2$ inch piece dalchini
1 tsp sonf
salt to taste

Fry the onions in ghee till golden brown. Remove and fry the semolina in the same karhai, till light brown. Then put in the bones and the remaining ingredients in a pressure-cooker with six cups of water. Add fried onions and semolina and cook at 15 lb pressure for half an hour. Strain and serve.

Serves : 4

DAHI BARA
(Meat Kababs in Curd)

The ingredients are the same as for Gular Kabab (without the filling) with the addition of

500 gm curd
$^1/_2$ tsp hing
4 hari mirch (finely
    chopped)

salt and lal mirch
    powder to taste
2 tsp sonf

Make the dahi baras according to the Gular Kabab recipe except that the form is flat, like a Shami Kabab and not round. Churn the curd till it becomes like thick cream. Add salt, lal and hari mirch, and add a little hing. A few minutes before serving, arrange the dahi baras in a plate and pour the curd over them. Lightly roast the hing and sonf on a tava, grind, and sprinkle over the dahi baras. Serve cold.

Makes : 16-20

Serves : 8-10

KHUBANI
(Meat Balls with Dried Apricots)

The ingredients are the same as the Gular Kabab, except for the filling, which is made up of

1 kg sugar (for syrup)	**40 pieces of kishmish**
20 badams or kaju	**300 gm ghee (for frying)**

In a karhai make a syrup of medium thick consistency with the sugar and four cups of water. If badams are used, soak them in hot water for some time, then skin. Shape the meat into round balls as you would Gular Kababs, putting in half a badam or kaju and one kishmish in the centre of each ball. Now fry the khubanis till they are golden brown and add them to the hot syrup, after removing the karhai from the fire. Allow to soak for half an hour before serving. Serve hot.

Note : To test the consistency of the syrup, dip a finger in the syrup and press the thumb and finger together. On separating, the syrup should form a thread.

Serves : 10-12

KACHCHE GOSHT KA PULAO
(Mutton Pulao)

1 kg meat (front leg,
breast or chops,
trimmed and cut into
good-sized pieces)
4 pieces of laung
2 tsp garam masala
1 inch piece ginger
(crushed)
a pinch of hing
1 kg Basmati rice

salt and lal mirch
powder to taste
100 gm ghee
25 gm kishmish
25 gm badam
10 choti elaichis
$1/2$ tsp shah zeera
a pinch of zafran
1 tsp keora water

Place meat in a degchi and cover with water till it stands half-inch above the meat. Tie together the laung, garam masala, ginger and hing in a muslin bag and add to the meat. Boil till the latter is tender. If no water remains, add a little more. Put in the rice, which should be soaked for at least two hours before cooking. (Normally one and a quarter time the volume of water is used when cooking rice. For instance, if the volume of soaked rice is four cups, then cook in five cups of water.) Add salt and lal mirch to taste, and cook till the rice is nearly done. Remove from fire.

Heat ghee and when hot, add kishmish, badam and elaichi. When the kishmish begins to swell, pour over the rice. Sprinkle with shah zeera and season with zafran ground to a paste with keora water. Now, carefully turn over the rice with the handle of a ladle, so that the rice grains do not break, and the zafran is well mixed with the rice.

Serves : 10

BIRYANI / BHUNE GOSHT KA PULAO
(Browned Mutton Pulao)

1 kg meat (dast or front leg)
300 gm ghee or vegetable oil
275 gm curd
salt to taste
4 pieces of laung
a pinch of hing
1 tsp sonth powder
1 tsp lal mirch powder (preferably roghni)
2 tsp garam masala
1 tsp sugar
1 inch piece dalchini
100 gm khoya
50 gm badam (soaked and skinned)
10 choti elaichis
25 gm kishmish
$1/_2$ tsp shah zeera
1 tsp keora water
a pinch of zafran
1 kg Basmati rice
2 inch piece ginger (ground)

Cook the meat as for Roghan Josh. Add one and a quarter times the volume of water (i.e. one cup of soaked rice to one and a quarter cups of water). Bring the cooked meat and water to a boil, and add the rice and remaining ingredients as in the Kachche Gosht ka Pulao. If preferred, make the rice first with the masala and, when nearly done, arrange alternate layers of meat and rice in another vessel, and place over a charcoal fire, covering the lid with live charcoal.

Variation : Biryani may also be made by adding golis of minced-meat, cooked earlier, to the rice.

Serves : 10

MACHHLI KHATTI
(Sour Fish)

1 kg fish (rohu or tingra)	100 gm curd
250 gm ghee or vegetable or mustard oil	1 tsp haldi
	1 tsp dhania powder
	2 tsp garam masala
a pinch of hing	2 tsp amchur powder
salt to taste	a bunch of hara dhania leaves (finely chopped)
1 inch piece ginger (crushed)	
$\frac{1}{4}$ tsp zeera	2 hari mirch (finely chopped)

Remove its head and tail and cut the fish, lengthwise, into two pieces. Remove intestines, etc., wash and clean. Scald the two pieces by plunging them in boiling water for two minutes. Drain, remove skin, cut into two-inch pieces and deep fry in ghee or oil till golden brown.

Set aside the fried fish and fry the hing, ginger, zeera and curd in the remaining ghee till reddish brown. Now add haldi, the fish and half a cup of water. Simmer on low heat till tender. Then add dhania, garam masala, amchur, hara dhania, hari mirch and cook for another few minutes.

Serves : 6-8

MACHHLI DUM
(Baked Fish)

The ingredients and method are the same as for Machhli Khatti, except that no haldi or amchur is used. If desired, peeled and fried potatoes may be added to the fish.

Serves : 6-8

MACHHLI TALI
(Fried Fish)

1 kg fish (tingra or
  pomfret)
salt and lal mirch
  powder to taste

15 gm curd
1 tblsp vinegar
200 gm ghee

Skin and cut the fish into half-inch thick and three to four inch long pieces. (If pomfret is used, cut lengthwise, into two pieces only.) Wash and drain. Dip the fish into a mixture of salt, lal mirch, curd and vinegar and set aside for an hour.

Before frying, squeeze the fish in order to drain the surplus mixture, and fry till golden brown. If desired, the fish may be coated with breadcrumbs and beaten egg white, before frying.

Serves : 6-8

MACHHLI KE KOFTE
(Fish Rolls)

1 kg fish (tingra or
   singhara)
250 gm ghee or
   vegetable oil
6 medium potatoes
2 tsp dhania powder
salt and lal mirch
   powder to taste

2 medium onions
2 eggs
1 tsp lemon juice
a bunch of hara dhania
   leaves (finely chopped)
25 gm rice flour or
   breadcrumbs

Clean the fish and cut it into three-inch pieces. Boil for a couple of minutes till tender. Drain and cool. Skin and remove the bones, if any, and mash, either with a fork or with your hands.

Boil the potatoes, cool, peel and mash. Mix in with the fish, and add dhania, salt and lal mirch. In a karhai, heat one tablespoon of ghee, and put in the fish and potato mixture. Stir till the moisture is absorbed, taking care not to burn it. Remove and set aside.

Fry the onions till brown and add to the fish after straining the fat. Break the eggs over the fish and mix well; add lemon juice. Mix lightly till uniform. Sprinkle over with hara dhania and form into koftas (three inches long and three-quarters of an inch thick). Roll in breadcrumbs or rice flour, and deep fry till they are uniformly light brown.

Serves : 8

MACHHLI TAMATAR
(Fish in Tomato Curry)

1 kg fish (tingra or
  singhara)
$^1/_2$ kg ripe tomatoes
a pinch of hing
$^1/_4$ tsp zeera
2 medium onions (finely
  chopped)
salt and lal mirch
  powder to taste
$^1/_2$ tsp sonth

1 tsp dhania powder
$^1/_2$ tsp semolina
$^1/_2$ tsp ginger (crushed)
2 hari mirch (finely
  chopped)
a bunch of hara dhania
  leaves (finely chopped)
100 gm ghee or
  vegetable oil

Clean and cut the fish into three-inch pieces. Boil till tender, drain and cool. Skin and remove bones, if any, and break into pieces. Boil tomatoes in a little water, cool, skin and mash till pulpy.

Heat the ghee, add hing, zeera and onions. Fry till brown, add the tomato pulp, salt, lal mirch and the remaining ingredients. When the tomato pulp thickens, add the fish. Place on low heat and cook for ten minutes. (The gravy should not be too dry.) Season with hara dhania and serve.

Serves : 6-8

MURGH MUSSALLAM
(Whole Chicken Stuffed and Baked)

1 kg chicken (dressed)
50 gm Basmati rice
1 tsp sonth powder
2 inch piece ginger
8 peppercorns
6 cloves garlic
3 medium onions
2 tsp garam masala
1 tsp sugar
250 gm curd

salt and lal mirch
　　powder to taste
250 gm ghee or
　　vegetable oil
a pinch of hing
15 gm badam
25 gm kishmish
15 gm chironji
100 gm khoya
1 tsp khuskhus

Soak the rice in water for an hour and strain. Then grind together all the ingredients (except salt and lal mirch, hing, badam, kishmish, chironji and khoya) with a little curd. Now fork the chicken and smear it with the remaining curd and the ground masalas.

Heat 50 gms of ghee and fry the strained rice for three to four minutes, stirring all the time. Add salt, lal mirch, hing, badam, kishmish, chironji and khoya. Pour in a cup of water and cook the rice till it is half done. Stuff the chicken with this mixture and tie securely with a thread to prevent the ingredients from spilling out. Place the chicken in a degchi with the remaining ghee and half a cup of water, over a charcoal fire, covering the lid with live charcoals. Cook till the water is absorbed and the meat is tender.

Serves : 8

MURGH DUM
(Baked Chicken)

Use 1 kg chicken (dressed and cut into pieces) and the same ingredients and method as for Mutton Qorma.

Serves : 6

MURGH QALIA
(Chicken in Turmeric Gravy)

Use 1 kg chicken (dressed and cut into pieces) and the same ingredients and method as for Mutton Qalia.

Serves : 6

Kashmiri Muslim Recipes

TRAMI MURGH KOKUR
(Saffron Chicken)

1 kg chicken	2 tsp lal mirch powder
2 handi-spoonfuls ghee	4 sticks dalchini
4 tblsp onion paste*	1 gm zafran
2 tsp sonth	salt to taste
10 pieces of laung	5 tsp sonf

Slice the chicken in two along the middle and clip the wings and neck. Deep fry the pieces in ghee till they turn slightly brown. Remove from ghee and set aside.

Put two tablespoons of the remaining ghee in a handi, add four cups of meat stock, all the chicken pieces and the masalas, except zafran, and boil. When it begins to simmer, make a paste of the zafran (with water) and add it to the dish. Simmer it till dry.

Trami murgh is served dry.

*Onion paste is generally made from Kashmiri meadow onions which are locally called 'pran'. If eaten raw, they can burn the palate or one could even lose one's voice for a temporary period. The onion is chopped into small pieces, fried till golden brown and then ground into a paste. The colour of the paste is a golden-yellowish-white. Invariably used in a wide variety of dishes, the paste has a unique fragrance which is peculiar to Kashmiri Muslim cooking.

Note : Meat stock is produced with bones from minced meat which is boiled with a little salt and garlic.

Serves : 2-4

TRAMI MURGH SAFED
(Chicken in White Sauce)

1 kg chicken	2 tsp sonth
4 cups milk	10 pieces of laung,
2 handi-spoonfuls ghee	5 sticks dalchini
5 tsp sonf (powdered)	salt to taste

Slice the chicken in two along the middle and clip the wings and the neck. Deep fry the pieces in ghee till they turn slightly brown.

Dilute the milk with a cup of water, add sonf and sonth. Put all the remaining ingredients and allow it to boil for three or four minutes. Now add the chicken and allow it to simmer till it is dry.

Serves : 2-4

RISTA
(Pounded Meat Balls in Onion Gravy)

1½ kg meat (fresh,
  boneless mutton pieces)
1 handi-spoonful ghee or
  oil
4 tblsp onion paste
  (made from 4 medium
  onions)
4 tsp sonth powder

2 tsp sonf (powdered)
1 tsp dalchini (powdered)
2 tsp lal mirch powder
6 bari elaichis (ground)
salt to taste
1 cup mowal extract* (or
  red edible colourant)

On a smooth-surfaced stone, pound the pieces of mutton with a wooden mallet till they turn to pulp. Add a pinch of sonth, salt, bari elaichi and continue pounding. Turn the pulp into round balls of about one and a quarter inch diameter. In a round-bottomed degchi, boil a litre of water and place the meat balls one by one in it. Stir them slowly for about five minutes. Remove the meat balls and set aside.

In a separate vessel, pour the ghee/oil and bring it to a

boil. Add all the ingredients except the onion paste. Add two cups of water and immerse the meat balls. Now add the onion paste to the mixture. While it is simmering, add a cupful of mowal and allow it to simmer further till the ghee/oil appears. The dish is now ready.

Note : Mowal is an

extract of cockscomb flowers used in several Kashmiri Muslim dishes as a colourant. The cockscomb flowers are harvested, dried in the shade and sold in the market by greengrocers. The extract is obtained by boiling the flowers in water and when they cool, by filtering them through a muslin cloth.

Serves : 6

GUSHTABA
(Pounded Meat Balls in Curd Gravy)

1½ kg meat (fresh, bone-less mutton pieces)	5 tsp sonth
1 handi-spoonful ghee/oil	2 tsp sonf (powdered)
1 tblsp onion paste (made from a medium onion)	4 sticks of dalchini
	6 bari elaichis (powdered)
	salt to taste
	1 kg curd

On a smooth-surfaced stone pound the pieces of mutton with a wooden mallet till they turn to pulp. Add a pinch of salt, a teaspoon of sonth, the bari elaichis and continue pounding. Turn the pulp into round balls two inches in diameter.

In a round-bottomed degchi, boil an adequate quantity of water and immerse the meat balls. Stir them slowly for about five minutes. Remove and set aside.

In a separate vessel put ghee/oil, add the curd and beat. Stir the mixture till the curd turns light brown. Add six cups of water and all the remaining ingredients and the meat balls. Boil for five minutes, then let it simmer for about fifteen minutes.

Note : Pounding meat is a laborious, time-consuming exercise. Any gadget which can grind the meat to a pulp would be advisable. Gadgets used for mincing meat, however, are not advisable.

Serves : 6

TABAK MAAZ
(Lamb Ribs)

1 kg meat (ribs only)*	1 tsp dalchini (powdered)
1 handi-spoonful ghee	4 pieces of laung
2 tsp sonth	$\frac{1}{2}$ tsp haldi
5 tsp sonf (powdered)	salt to taste

Take a litre of water in a vessel, add the ingredients and place the pieces of ribs one by one into the water and boil till the meat turns tender. Remove the pieces and set aside.

In a flat, non-stick pan arrange the rib pieces, add a scoop of ghee and place on low heat for about five minutes. Now turn the pieces upside down and continue cooking for another five minutes. Turn them again and feel the meat with your fingers to see if it has turned crisp. If so, remove from flame. At the time of serving, place the pan in an oven for about five minutes at a medium temperature and serve the dish hot.

*Take the entire rib section and cut into rectangular pieces across the ribs. Care should be taken that the muscle covering the ribs is not removed. Each piece of the rib should be about five inches in length and two inches in width, containing about three to four pieces of rib bone in the meat.

Serves : 6

AAB GOSH
(Mutton in Milk Sauce)

1 kg meat (preferably chops)	5 tsp sonf (whole)
1 kg milk	2 tsp sonth
1/2 handi-spoonful ghee	5 sticks dalchini
5 elaichis (whole)	4 pieces of laung
1 tblsp onion paste	1 tblsp peppercorns
4 cloves of garlic	salt to taste

Boil the meat in a litre of water, add sonf, garlic, salt and one teaspoon of sonth. Continue boiling till the meat turns tender. Keep it aside. In another vessel, boil the milk, add the elaichi till it thickens and becomes three-fourths of its volume. Add the other ingredients and continue boiling. Now add the meat. Take the remaining stock of the meat, filter it through a fine muslin cloth and add it to the dish. Continue boiling for about five minutes and then simmer for fifteen minutes. The dish is now ready.

Serves : 4

DANIWAL KORMA
(Mutton in Coriander Sauce)

1 kg meat (preferably
    pelvic region and tail)
1 handi-spoonful of ghee
½ kg curd
5 chopped onions (whole)
2 tsp sonth

2 tsp sonf (powdered)
3 tsp dhania powder
1 tsp peppercorns
salt to taste
a bunch of hara dhania
    leaves (finely chopped)

Heat the ghee in a vessel, add the curd and the chopped onions. Stir them together till they acquire a uniform consistency. Add the meat and the remaining ingredients, pour three cups of water and boil till the meat becomes tender. Allow it to simmer. Remove from heat. Garnish with hara dhania leaves.

Serves : 4

MARCHWANGAN KORMA / MIRCH KORMA
(Mutton in Hot Chilli Sauce)

1 kg meat (shoulder blade)	¹/₂ cup curd
1 handi-spoonful ghee/oil	20 lal mirch (whole)
4 tsp sonf (powdered)	4 choti elaichis
3 tsp dalchini (powdered)	4 pieces of laung
¹/₂ cup mowal extract or edible red colourant	¹/₂ tsp zeera (black)
	salt to taste
	2 tsp sonth

Soak the lal mirch in hot water for a couple of minutes, remove the seeds, add a cup of water and grind. Set aside.

Heat ghee/oil in a vessel, add curd and when it turns brown, put in the pieces of meat and stir for about four minutes. Now add the other ingredients. Filter the ground mirch through a fine muslin cloth and add the extract

gradually to the meat and stir. Finally add the mowal extract and allow it to simmer till the ghee/oil appears.

Note : The essence of this korma is dalchini. If the dish tastes very hot, add two tablespoons of tamarind extract and allow it to simmer.

Serves : 6

ALU BUKHARA KORMA
(Mutton in Plum Sauce)

1 kg meat (shoulder or
   hind leg)
1 handi-spoonful ghee/oil
4 tsp sonf (powdered)
2 tsp sonth
1 tsp dalchini (powdered)
$^1/_2$ cup curd
100 gm dried plums

$^1/_2$ tsp zeera
4 choti elaichis
$1^1/_2$ tsp lal mirch powder
salt to taste
1 cup mowal extract
4 tblsp badam (skinned
   and chopped into
   long pieces)

Soak the dried plums in hot water till they become tender, then remove the stones and set aside.

Heat ghee/oil in a vessel, add curd and stir till the curd turns brown. Add the plums and stir till they dissolve. Now put the meat in, stir for five minutes and add the rest of the ingredients. Pour two cups of water, add the mowal and boil till the meat becomes tender. Allow it to simmer. At the time of serving, garnish the dish with the chopped badam.

Serves : 4

<u>VEGETARIAN</u>

ALU MATAR
(Potatoes with Peas)

500 gm potatoes
65 gm ghee or
   vegetable oil
a pinch of hing
1 tsp zeera
$\frac{1}{4}$ tsp methi dana
2 pieces of laung
salt, lal mirch powder
   and hari mirch (finely
   chopped) to taste
1 tsp haldi (optional)

1 tsp sonth powder
1 tsp dhania powder
1 tsp succh bari
   (powdered)
a bunch of hara dhania
   leaves (finely chopped)
500 gms peas
100 gm fresh or dried
   fenugreek (optional)
2-3 tomatoes (optional)

Peel and cut the potatoes into medium-sized pieces. Fry lightly and set aside. Heat the ghee and splutter the hing, zeera, methi dana and laung. Add the vegetable you wish to mix with the potatoes (except tomatoes), and half a cup of water. Cover. Shake the vessel lightly every few minutes or stir carefully with a ladle so that the vegetable is well mixed without breaking. Add the remaining masalas and succh bari. When nearly done, add the fried potatoes. Sprinkle over with hara dhania.

If tomatoes are used, first scald them in hot water, then cool, peel and pulp. Pour into the vessel containing the potatoes a few minutes before the vegetable is done. Should you prefer fresh fenugreek, cut it fine and mix in with the masala as you would other vegetables. Fry till it emits a typical fenugreek aroma, add the potatoes, sprinkle a little water and allow to simmer for a few minutes. For dry fenugreek, use two tablespoonfuls with the fried potatoes. Sprinkle a little water, mix well and allow to simmer for a few minutes till done.

Variation : This dish can be made as a gravy or as a combination with cauliflower, cabbage, tomatoes or fenugreek.

Serves : 6-8

ALU AUR KELE KI BHUJIA
(Spiced Potatoes and Bananas in Curd)

6 raw bananas	$^1/_2$ tsp zeera
6 medium potatoes	$^1/_4$ tsp methi dana
100 gm ghee or	$^1/_2$ tsp sonth powder
vegetable oil	$^1/_2$ tsp succh or petha
a pinch of hing	bari (powdered)
salt, lal mirch powder	$^1/_2$ tsp dhania powder
and hari mirch (finely	60 gm curd (beaten)
chopped) to taste	a bunch of hara dhania
$^1/_4$ tsp kalonji	leaves (finely chopped)

Peel the bananas and cut into rounds, half an inch thick. Peel the potatoes and cut into fours. Fry both to a golden brown in the ghee in batches.

Heat the ghee and splutter the hing, zeera, methi dana, and then add the fried bananas, potatoes and the remaining masalas. Shake the vessel a couple of times and add half a cup of water. Cover and allow to simmer for ten to fifteen minutes. When soft, add the beaten curd, cover and place on a very slow fire for another ten minutes. Remove and sprinkle with finely chopped hara dhania.

Serves : 6-8

KHATTE ALU OR ARVI
(Sour Potatoes or Yam)

1 kg potatoes or yam
150 gm oil (preferably
    mustard)
a pinch of hing
1 tsp zeera
2 pieces of laung
$\frac{1}{4}$ tsp methi dana
salt and lal mirch
    powder to taste
1 tsp haldi powder
1 tsp sonth powder

2 hari mirch (finely
    chopped)
1 inch piece ginger
    (crushed)
2 tsp amchur powder
1 tsp dhania powder
1 inch piece succh bari
    (powdered)
a bunch of hara dhania
    leaves (finely chopped)

Peel and cut the potatoes into one-inch by half-inch pieces. If yam is used, peel and slice it lengthwise into two, and fry lightly. (Potatoes need not be fried.) Smoke the oil and splutter the hing, zeera, laung and methi dana. Add the potatoes or fried yam, salt, lal and hari mirch, sonth and ginger. Fry for five minutes, add haldi, stir for a minute and add enough water to cover the vegetables and allow to simmer till soft. Add amchur, dhania and succh bari and simmer for another few minutes. Remove, and garnish with hara dhania.

Serves : 8-10

ARVI KE PATTE
(Spiced Mixture wrapped in Yam Leaves)

250 gm urad dal (dhuli)
12 medium-sized yam
   leaves
salt, lal mirch powder
   and hari mirch (finely
   chopped) to taste
2 tsp zeera
a pinch of hing
1 tsp sonth powder

1 inch piece ginger
   (crushed)
1 tsp dhania powder
250 gm oil
1 tsp haldi powder
2 tsp amchur powder
a bunch of hara dhania
   or pudina leaves
   (finely chopped)

Soak dal for two hours, drain and grind to a thin paste. Wash and cut the central stems of the yam leaves, and lay them, on an inverted thali. Mix the masalas, except amchur and haldi, into the dal paste and smear the mixture lightly over each leaf. Roll the leaves from end to end to make into flat one-inch rolls. Place them on a board and cut into two-inch pieces and cover the ends of each with more paste. When all the pieces are done, fry three or four at a time till they turn golden brown. Set aside.

In another vessel, put in the remaining oil, add two cups of water and boil. As it boils, put in the haldi, add the fried yam leaves and allow to simmer till they are tender, but not too soft as they may break. When a little gravy is left, add the amchur and shake the vessel lightly. Remove from heat. Sprinkle over with hara dhania or pudina.

Serves : 10-12

BAIGAN
(Spiced Brinjal and Potatoes)

4 brinjals
6 medium potatoes
125 gm oil (preferably
    mustard)
salt, lal mirch powder
    and hari mirch (finely
    chopped) to taste
1 tsp dhania powder
1 inch piece ginger
    (crushed)
1 tsp succh bari
    (powdered)

$^1/_2$ tsp sonth powder
1 tsp haldi
a pinch of hing
$^1/_4$ tsp methi dana
1 tsp zeera
100 gm beans
4 tomatoes
2 onions
50 gm fresh fenugreek
a bunch of hara dhania
    leaves (finely chopped)

Peel and slice the brinjals and potatoes into one and a half inch pieces. If beans are used, cut into half-inch pieces, after stripping the veins on either side. Should you prefer fenugreek, cut it fine. If tomatoes, slice them into fours, and if onions, cut them into half-inch thick pieces.

Any of the above combinations of vegetables with brinjal may be cooked in the following ways:

Either fry all the vegetables lightly in oil, except the tomatoes and fenugreek, or put all the vegetables in together and fry till done. In either case, add the masalas after the vegetables are fried. If the potatoes are not quite done, add a little water and simmer for some time till done. Add hari mirch, sprinkle over with the hara dhania, cover and cook till ready. If you wish to have sour brinjal, add two teaspoons of amchur powder.

Serves : 6-8

BAIGAN MASALEDAAR
(Spiced Brinjal Slices)

6 brinjals (medium, round)
125 gm oil (preferably
  mustard)
salt to taste
1 tsp dhania powder
1 tsp garam masala
  powder

2 tsp amchur powder
1 tsp lal mirch powder
$\frac{1}{2}$ tsp sonth powder
a pinch of hing (roasted
  and powdered)
a bunch of hara dhania
  leaves (finely chopped)

Wash and peel the brinjals. Cut into rounds a quarter of an inch thick, and fry till light brown. Now remove the brinjals from the vessel and arrange them on a plate. Mix all the ingredients together and sprinkle over the brinjals. Now place another layer of brinjals over this and sprinkle over with masalas again. Finally, garnish with hara dhania.

Serves : 6-8

CHUKANDAR
(Beetroot Curry)

$^1/_2$ kg beetroot
100 gm ghee or
    vegetable oil
2 pieces of laung
a pinch of hing
$^1/_4$ tsp methi dana
$^1/_2$ tsp zeera
$^1/_2$ tsp sonth powder
1 tsp dhania powder

salt, lal mirch powder
    and hari mirch (finely
    chopped) to taste
1 tsp succh or petha bari
    (powdered)
250 gm tomatoes
    (optional)
a bunch of hara dhania
    leaves (finely chopped)

Wash the beetroot well, peel and cut into quarter-inch thick pieces. Finely chop the leaves as well, as they are used in this preparation.

Heat the oil, and splutter the laung, hing, zeera and methi dana. Put in the beetroot. Fry a little, add a cup of water and cover. As this vegetable takes a long time to cook, tomatoes should not be added till it is tender. When half done, add the remaining masalas. Pour another half cup of water or more if necessary, so that there is some gravy. Cook till done and garnish with hara dhania. This makes a colourful dish when eaten with plain rice.

Serves : 4-6

CUT CHAMAN
(Sliced Cottage Cheese Curry)

500 gm chaman
250 gm potatoes
  (medium sized)
125 gm ghee or
  vegetable oil
salt, lal mirch powder
  and hari mirch (finely
  chopped) to taste
2 tsp garam masala

1 tsp succh bari
  (powdered)
1 tsp zeera
a pinch of hing
1 tsp sonth powder
1 tsp dhania powder
1 tsp haldi powder
a bunch of hara dhania
  leaves (finely chopped)

Cut the chaman into half-inch cubes. Peel and cut the potatoes the same size. Fry them separately till they are golden brown. Do not overfry chaman. Heat the ghee and put in the fried chaman and potatoes, together with all the ingredients except hara dhania. Add one and a half cups of water. Allow to simmer on a slow fire for about ten minutes till the potatoes turn soft. Sprinkle over with hara dhania when there is a little gravy left.

Serves : 10-12

MATAR CHAMAN
(Peas and Cottage Cheese Curry)

500 gm chaman
150 gm ghee or
  vegetable oil
a pinch of hing
4 pieces of laung
1 tsp zeera
250 gm peas (shelled)
1 tsp sonth
1 tsp haldi

salt, lal mirch powder
  and hari mirch (finely
  chopped) to taste
1 tsp dhania powder
1 inch piece ginger
  (crushed)
1 tsp garam masala
a bunch of hara dhania
  leaves (finely chopped)

Cut the chaman into one-inch cubes. Fry lightly for about two minutes. Remove and set aside. In a degchi put in the remaining ghee and splutter the hing, laung and zeera. Next, add the peas and sufficient water and cook for five minutes. Put in the remaining masalas. When the peas are tender, add the fried chaman. Garnish with finely chopped hara dhania. This dish has very little gravy.

Serves : 8-10

METHI CHAMAN
(Fenugreek and Cottage Cheese Curry)

50 gm fresh fenugreek or
    25 gm dehydrated
    fenugreek (boiled)
500 gm chaman
150 gm ghee or
    vegetable oil
a pinch of hing
4 pieces of laung
1 tsp zeera
$1/_2$ tsp haldi
1 tsp dhania power

$1/_2$ tsp sonth
salt, lal mirch powder
    and hari mirch (finely
    chopped) to taste
1 inch piece ginger
    (crushed)
$1/_2$ tsp garam masala
50 gm spinach
or 125 gm brinjal
or 125 gm snake-gourd

Grind the fenugreek (or spinach) finely on a stone and set aside. Cut the chaman into medium-thick one-inch square pieces (or larger, if desired) and fry till light brown. Set aside.

In the remaining oil, splutter the hing, laung, zeera, add the ground fenugreek and fry. Keep stirring till it emits a strong aroma. Add haldi, sonth, salt, lal mirch, ginger, dhania powder and one and a half cups of water. As the mixture begins to thicken, add the fried chaman and keep the vessel over a slow fire. Allow to simmer for ten minutes, making sure that the gravy is thick. Add garam masala a few minutes before removing. Garnish with hara dhania.

Variation : If brinjal or snake gourd is used, peel and cut into slices. Fry lightly and set aside. Add the same when placing the chaman in the vessel and cook as directed above.

Serves : 6-8

DUM ALU
(Baked Spiced Potatoes in Rich Gravy)

1 kg potatoes (medium sized)
250 gm oil (preferably mustard)
150 gm ghee
salt to taste
a pinch of hing
4 pieces of laung
1 tsp zeera
2 hari mirch (finely chopped)

1 tsp lal mirch powder
2 tsp dhania powder
1 inch piece ginger (crushed)
1 tsp sonth powder
1 tsp sugar
1 tsp garam masala (heaped)
125 gm curd (whipped)
a bunch of hara dhania leaves (finely chopped)

Potatoes are generally of two kinds, pahari and desi. If desi potatoes are used, boil them till they can be pierced easily with a fork. Drain, cool and peel. If the pahari variety are used, simply peel without boiling. Pierce each all over with a fine knitting needle or toothpick.

Heat oil in a karhai, and put in the potatoes, till half the vessel is full. Gently turn them till they are uniformly brown. When half done, sprinkle a little salt water over them. This ensures uniform distribution of the salt and softens the potatoes. When the potatoes are fried, remove from fire, drain and set aside.

In a separate vessel, heat the ghee and splutter the hing, laung, zeera and hari mirch. Stir for a few seconds, then add potatoes, salt (if more is desired), lal mirch, dhania and two cups of water. Next put in the ginger, sonth and sugar. Bring to a boil, allow to boil for a few minutes, and then place the vessel on a charcoal fire, add the curd and garam masala and place live coals on the lid. When the water evaporates and ghee appears on the surface, the dish is ready. Garnish with hara dhania and serve.

Note : Desi potatoes are preferred for this preparation.

Serves : 8-10

DUM ARVI
(Spicy Baked Yam)

1 kg yam, (preferably   the same ingredients as
    3 inches in size) and   for Dum Alu

Boil the yam in water till soft. Strain and cool, then peel. Prick it all over with a toothpick or fine knitting needle. Follow the recipe for Dum Alu for the rest.

Serves : 8-10

DUM BANDA
(Spicy Baked Yam)

500-700 gm yam (8 or 9   salt, lal mirch powder
    inches in size)   and hari mirch (finely
200 gms ghee or   chopped) to taste
    vegetable oil   1 tsp dhania powder
a pinch of hing   1 tsp succh bari
$1/_2$ tsp zeera   (powdered)
2 pieces of laung   1 inch piece ginger
1 tsp sonth powder   (crushed)

Peel and cut the yams into squares two by two inches and half an inch thick. Fry till light brown. Set aside. Splutter the hing, zeera, laung and sonth in the remaining oil and add ginger. Add a cup of water and put in the fried yams. Allow to simmer for fifteen minutes till the pieces are soft, then add the remaining masalas, cover and cook for a few minutes more.

Variation : This vegetable can be made sour by adding one teaspoon of haldi to the masalas and two' tablespoons of amchur with the water. Put in an extra pinch of salt and a little sugar. Garnish with hara dhania or pudina.

Serves : 6-8

DUM BHINDI
(Spicy Baked Okra)

$\frac{1}{2}$ kg okra	salt, lal mirch powder
125 gm oil (preferably	and hari mirch (finely
mustard)	chopped) to taste
a pinch of hing	2 tsp succh or petha bari
2 pieces of laung	(powdered)
1 tsp zeera	1 inch piece ginger
$\frac{1}{4}$ tsp methi dana	(crushed)
$\frac{1}{4}$ tsp kalonji	a bunch of hara dhania
1 tsp dhania powder	leaves (finely chopped)
$\frac{1}{2}$ tsp sonth powder	1 tsp haldi powder

Wash the okras well, dry thoroughly with a piece of cloth and cut the top and tail. Slit them about an inch, lengthwise. Heat oil in a frying pan or karhai, and fry the okras (eight or ten at a time, depending on the size of the karhai) till they are light brown. Set aside.

Remove the excess oil and splutter the hing, laung, zeera, methi dana, kalonji and ginger and add the fried okra. Next, add the remaining masalas and a little water. Toss the okra in a the vessel lightly. Do not use a ladle as it will crush the vegetable. Allow to simmer till it is done, then garnish with hara dhania.

Variation : Fried potatoes may be added at the time the fried okra is put in.

Serves : 4-5

DUM KATHAL
(Spicy Baked Jackfruit)

750 gm jackfruit (with
　large seeds, skinned)
300 gm potatoes
250 gm mustard oil
100 gm ghee or
　vegetable oil
a pinch of hing
$\frac{1}{2}$ tsp zeera
$\frac{1}{2}$ tsp methi dana
1 tsp sonth powder

salt, lal mirch powder
　and hari mirch (finely
　chopped) to taste
1 inch piece ginger
　(ground)
1 tsp succh bari
　(powdered)
1 tsp garam masala
a bunch of hara dhania
　leaves (finely chopped)

Slice the jackfruit into three inches long by one and a half inch wide pieces and peel off the outer comb. Peel and cut the potatoes in twos. Fry both in mustard oil till they turn golden brown and set aside.

Heat ghee in a vessel, and splutter the hing, zeera and methi dana. Next, put in the fried jackfruit and potatoes and add all the remaining ingredients, except hara dhania, and two cups of water. Shake the vessel frequently and let the vegetables simmer for fifteen minutes. When the jackfruit and potatoes are soft to the touch, add the hara dhania.

Variation : Jackfruit can be made sour by adding two tablespoons of either amchur, lemon juice or tomato pulp, and one teaspoon of haldi.

Serves : 8-10

DUM KARELA
(Spicy Baked Bitter Gourd)

10 pieces of bitter gourd
100 gm mustard or any
  other oil
100 gm ghee
10 medium potatoes
a pinch of hing
1 tsp zeera
$1/4$ tsp methi dana
$1/4$ tsp kalonji
$1/2$ tsp sonth powder
1 tsp sonf

salt, lal mirch powder
  and hari mirch (finely
  chopped) to taste
1 tsp succh bari
  (powdered)
1 inch piece ginger
  (crushed)
1 tsp dhania powder
a bunch of hara dhania
  leaves (finely chopped)

Scrape the bitter gourds and cut them into fours, lengthwise. Remove the seeds, wash and fry in mustard oil till light brown. Fry the potatoes, likewise. In another vessel, heat the ghee and splutter the hing, zeera, methi dana and kalonji. After a few seconds, add the bitter gourds and potatoes. Put in half a cup of water and add the rest of the spices and ginger. Allow to simmer for fifteen minutes. When soft, add the hara dhania. Shake the vessel often to mix the spices evenly. Cover and keep on a very slow fire till all the water has evaporated.

Serves : 10-12

DUM LAUKI
(Spicy Baked Bottle Gourd)

1 kg bottle gourd
100 gm ghee or vegetable
    oil
a pinch of hing
1/2 tsp zeera
salt, lal mirch powder
    and hari mirch (finely
    chopped) to taste
1/4 tsp methi dana

1 tsp succh bari
    (powdered)
1 tsp sonth powder
1 inch piece ginger
    (ground)
1 tsp dhania powder
a bunch of hara dhania
    leaves (finely chopped)

Peel and cut the bottle gourd into one and a half inch by one inch pieces. In a vessel, heat the ghee and splutter the zeera, hing and methi dana. Add the bottle gourd and cover. Do not add water, as it releases abundant water. Cook on a slow fire. After it has turned soft, add the rest of the spices and hara dhania, and cover.

Variations : Bottle gourd can also be made as a bhujia. For this purpose, it should be cut fine. Use coarsely ground black pepper instead of lal mirch and sprinkle over only when the vegetable is almost done. Use 50 gm of oil or ghee only.

Bottle gourd with whipped curd is another delicacy. In this recipe, one teaspoon haldi should be added in with the spices. The curd is whipped and added to the cooking dish when the vegetable is almost done. Garnish with hara dhania.

Bottle gourd may also be combined with potatoes, fenugreek or tomatoes.

Serves : 4-6

DUM NADRU
(Spicy Baked Lotus Roots)

$^1/_2$ kg lotus roots
$^1/_2$ kg potatoes (optional)
$^1/_2$ kg peas (optional)
150 gm ghee or oil
  (preferably mustard)
a pinch of hing
4 pieces of laung
1 tsp zeera
2 hari mirch (finely
  chopped)

1 tsp lal mirch powder
2 tsp dhania powder
1 inch piece ginger
  (crushed)
1 tsp sonth powder
2 tsp sugar
1 tsp garam masala
a bunch of hara dhania
  leaves (finely chopped)
salt to taste

Cut the lotus roots diagonally. Wash well, to clean out the dirt from its cavities. Peel and cut the potatoes into twos, and shell the peas.

Fry the lotus roots and potatoes till light brown and set aside. In the remaining oil, splutter the hing, laung, zeera and add the lotus roots, potatoes and peas. Add a cup of salt water and the rest of the spices. Allow to simmer for fifteen minutes till soft. The vessel should be lifted and the vegetables tossed lightly from time to time. When done, garnish with hara dhania.

Serves : 10-12

DUM PARWAL
(Spicy Baked Gherkins)

12 large gherkins
12 small potatoes
   (optional)
125 gm ghee or
   vegetable oil
a pinch of hing
4 pieces of laung
salt, lal mirch powder
   and hari mirch (finely
   chopped) to taste

$^1/_2$ tsp zeera
1 tsp sonth powder
1 inch piece ginger
   (ground)
1 tsp garam masala
1 tsp dhania powder
$^1/_2$ tsp succh bari
   (powdered)
a bunch of hara dhania
   leaves (finely chopped)

Scrape the skin off the gherkins. Peel the potatoes and cut them in twos, lengthwise. Slit the gherkins down one side and remove the seeds. Fry both in oil till light brown and set aside. Heat the ghee in a vessel, and splutter the hing, laung and zeera, then add the fried gherkins and potatoes. Pour in a cup of water and allow to simmer for fifteen minutes. Now add salt and the rest of the masalas. When the two vegetables are soft to touch, sprinkle over the hara dhania.

Variation : Should you prefer this dish with gravy, use a teaspoon of haldi, add a little more water, half a teaspoon of flour, and cook.

Serves : 10-12

DUM RATALU
(Spicy Baked Yam)

$^1/_2$ kg yam
150 gm ghee or
    vegetable oil
a pinch of hing
4 pieces of laung
$^1/_2$ tsp zeera
salt, lal mirch powder
    and hari mirch (finely
    chopped) to taste

1 tsp garam masala
$^1/_2$ tsp succh bari
    (powdered)
$^1/_2$ tsp sonth powder
1 inch piece ginger
    (ground)
125 gm curd
a bunch of hara dhania
    leaves (finely chopped)

Peel the yam, slice into rounds half an inch thick, and fry lightly in oil. Set aside. In the remaining oil, splutter the hing, zeera and laung. Add the yam, salt and the rest of the spices. Pour in a cup of water and allow to simmer for fifteen to twenty minutes till the yam becomes soft.

Whip the curd to a creamy consistency and add it to the yam when it is nearly done. Garnish with hara dhania.

Serves : 4-6

DUM TINDA
(Spicy Baked Gourd)

$^1/_2$ kg gourd (medium)
125 gm ghee or
    vegetable oil
a pinch of hing
2 pieces of laung
salt, lal mirch powder
    and hari mirch (finely
    chopped) to taste

$^1/_4$ tsp methi dana
1 tsp dhania powder
1 tsp succh bari
$^1/_2$ tsp sonth powder
1 inch piece ginger
    (crushed)
a bunch of hara dhania
    leaves (finely chopped)

Scrape and cut the gourds into fours. Heat the oil and

spluffer the hing, laung, zeera and methi dana. Add
the gourds, salt and lal mirch. Mix well with a ladle. Add
a little water, if required, as this vegetable is prepared
without gravy, and add the rest of the masalas. The
dish is ready as soon as the gourds become tender.
Garnish with hara dhania.

Variation : Should you prefer a combination of gourd
and potatoes, peel, cut and fry the potatoes separately
till they turn light brown. Add a little water to prevent
them from burning. When they are ready, mix them
with the rest of the ingredients and the gourds. Add a
quarter cup of water, cover, and cook for about ten
minutes, till done.

Serves : 4-6

DUM ZAMINKAND
(Spicy Baked Yam)

$1/2$ kg yam
125 gm ghee or
   vegetable oil
a few tamarind leaves
a pinch of hing
2 pieces of laung
salt, lal mirch powder
   and hari mirch (finely
   chopped) to taste

1 inch piece ginger
   (ground)
$1/2$ tsp sonth powder
1 tsp garam masala
$1/2$ tsp succh bari
1 tsp dhania powder
a bunch of hara dhania
   leaves (finely chopped)
$1/2$ tsp zeera

Peel the yam and cut it into two inches by one and a
half inch slices. To remove the sting, boil the cut
vegetable in water and tamarind leaves.

Drain the boiled yam and fry in hot oil till it turns golden
brown. Remove it from the vessel and set aside. While the

oil is still hot, splutter the hing, zeera and laung. Pour in a cup of water, then add the fried yam, salt, and the rest of the spices. Allow to simmer for fifteen minutes till the water evaporates. Garnish with hara dhania.

Variation : This vegetable may be made sour by adding one tablespoon of amchur and one teaspoon of haldi.

Note : Yam usually creates an itching sensation in the fingers; use a little oil to prevent this irritation. Ahmedabadi yam is preferred, as this does not cause itching or irritation.

Serves : 4-6

KHOYA MATAR
(Peas with Thickened Milk)

500 gm khoya
250 gm peas (shelled)
125 gm ghee or
    vegetable oil
a pinch of hing
4 pieces of laung
salt, lal mirch powder
    and hari mirch (finely
    chopped) to taste
1 tsp sonth powder

1 tsp zeera
1 tsp dhania powder
1 tsp garam masala
1 tsp succh bari
    (powdered)
1 inch piece ginger
    (crushed)
a bunch of hara dhania
    leaves (finely chopped)

Heat ghee in a degchi, splutter the hing, zeera, laung and khoya and fry on a slow fire till the khoya becomes reddish brown. Then add the peas, salt, the remaining spices and water (approximately two cups). Cook till the peas turn soft. Sprinkle over with hara dhania, cover, and cook for five minutes.

Serves : 10-12

LOBHIA
(Dry String Beans)

$^1/_2$ kg string beans
100 gm oil
a pinch of hing
$^1/_2$ tsp zeera
2 pieces of laung
salt, lal mirch powder
and hari mirch (finely
chopped) to taste

$^1/_4$ tsp methi dana
1 tsp dhania powder
1 tsp succh or petha bari
(ground)
1 tsp sonth powder,
a bunch of hara dhania
leaves (finely chopped)

Cut the string beans into half-inch pieces. Heat oil and splutter the hing, zeera, methi dana and laung. Add the string beans. Fry till it changes colour slightly. Add the salt and masàlas and fry a little more. Put in a quarter cup of water and allow to simmer till soft. Garnish with hara dhania.

Variation : Should you wish to add potatoes either cut and fry them lightly or put them in raw with the string beans and fry for some time before adding the water. There should be no gravy as this vegetable is served dry.

Serves : 4-6

KHATTI BHINDI
(Sour Okra with Gravy)

Ingredients are the same as for Dum Bhindi.

This vegetable is prepared and cooked in the same way as Dum Bhindi, except that one teaspoon of haldi is added with the masala and two teaspoons of amchur powder are added when the okra is nearly cooked. This dish should have some gravy. In place of amchur, tomatoes, lemon juice or raw green mangoes (ground finely), could be substituted.

Serves : 4-6

BHINDI KI BHUJIA
(Spicy Fried Okra)

Ingredients are the same as for Dum Bhindi.

Wash the okra well, rub dry with a piece of cloth, and cut the top and tail. Cut into half-inch rounds and fry in oil till light brown.

Reduce the quantity of oil and put in the okra and masalas. Sprinkle over with some water and cover. (Do not use a ladle as it will damage the okra.) Shake the vessel a few times, and add hara dhania.

Variation : If you wish to add potatoes, peel and cut them into half-inch pieces. Fry, and add them together with the okra and masalas.

Note : Never wash cut okra as water gets into the cavities and causes difficulties at the time of frying.

Serves : 4-6

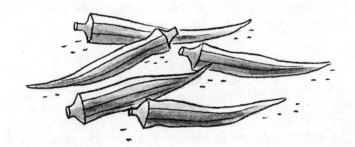

ALU OR KELE KI TIKIA
(Potato or Banana Kababs)

15 potatoes
125 gm ghee or
   vegetable oil
2 medium onions (finely
   chopped)
salt, lal mirch powder
   and hari mirch (finely
   chopped) to taste
1 tsp garam masala
1 tsp amchur powder

2 tsp dhania powder
1 inch piece ginger
   (ground)
a bunch of hara dhania
   leaves (finely chopped)
2 tblsp breadcrumbs
   arrowroot or cornflour
6 raw bananas (boiled
   and mashed)

Boil potatoes/bananas till soft; cool and peel. Mash well so as to make an even mass. Fry onions till they become a dark brown. Mix the onions in with the potatoes/bananas, masalas and hara dhania. (Dhania may be substituted with finely cut pudina leaves, dry or fresh.)

Make one-inch balls of the mashed potatoes/bananas (or larger, if preferred) and flatten them with your palms. Dust with arrowroot or breadcrumbs and fry two or three at a time.

Serves : 8-10

KATHAL KE KABAB
(Jackfruit Kababs)

The ingredients are the same as for the previous recipe (except potatoes and raw bananas) with the addition of

1 kg jackfruit
2 inch piece dalchini

250 gm chana dal

Peel the comb of the jackfruit and cut into two by two inch pieces. Wash dal and put it in a pressure-cooker with the jackfruit and dalchini. Pour in two cups of water and boil till the jackfruit and dal are both soft and dry. When cool, grind both on a stone.

Fry onions, and mix them in with all the masalas, salt and hara dhania. Mix this with the ground jackfruit and dal and form into kababs, round, oval or long. Cover with corn-flour or breadcrumbs and fry in hot ghee till they are golden brown. Serve hot.

Note : Kathal kababs are usually made from the small variety of jackfruit, which has very small seeds.

Serves : 8-10

ARVI KE KABAB
(Yam Kababs)

$1/_2$ kg yam
1 onion (optional)
100 gm ghee or
    vegetable oil
salt, lal mirch powder
    and hari mirch (finely
    chopped) to taste
$1/_2$ tsp sonth powder
1 inch piece ginger
    (crushed)

a pinch of hing (roasted)
$1/_2$ tsp garam masala
50 gm roasted gram
    (powdered)
1 tsp dhania powder
60 gm breadcrumbs or
    cornflour
a bunch of hara dhania
    leaves (finely chopped)

Boil the yam till soft; peel and mash. Cut and fry the onions till brown. Mix in the salt, masalas, hara dhania, hari mirch, ginger, fried onion and mashed yam. Form the mixture into kababs and coat with breadcrumbs or cornflour. Deep fry the kababs till they are golden brown.

Serves : 4-6

LOBHIA KE KABAB
(Bean Seed Kababs)

The ingredients are the same as in the previous recipe (except for yam) with the addition of :

**500 gm lobhia seeds
  (dehydrated)**

Soak the lobhia overnight. Next day, drain and grind. Use the same masalas as for Arvi ke Kabab, form the mixture into kababs and deep fry.

Serves : 4-6

ZAMINKAND KE KABAB
(Yam Kababs)

The ingredients are the same as for Alu ki Tikia. Instead of potatoes, use :

¹/₂ kg yam

Peel and cut the yam into one and a half inch slices. Fry in ghee till light brown. Grind finely and mix in the masalas as in Alu ki Tikia. Coat with arrowroot or breadcrumbs and deep fry.

Serves : 4-6

GANTH GOBHI
(Diced Knol Khol in Masala)

$^1/_2$ kg knol khol
125 gm ghee or
   vegetable oil
a pinch of hing
$^1/_2$ tsp zeera
$^1/_4$ tsp methi dana
2 pieces of laung
salt, lal mirch powder
   and hari mirch (finely
   chopped) to taste
1 tsp dhania powder

1 tsp garam masala
1 tsp succh bari
   (powdered)
1 tsp sonth powder
1 tsp haldi powder
1 inch piece ginger
   (crushed)
$^1/_2$ tsp sugar
a bunch of hara dhania
   leaves (finely chopped)

Peel and cut the knol khol into fours. Heat the ghee and splutter the hing, zeera, methi dana and laung. Add the knol khol. Shake the vessel, cover and allow to simmer for ten minutes. Add a tablespoon or two of water to prevent it from burning. Cover. Put in the remaining ingredients (except sugar and hara dhania) and fry for two or three minutes. Add a cup of water and allow to simmer on a slow fire for another fifteen minutes till it is soft. Add sugar, hara dhania and continue to cook on a slow fire till the water has very nearly evaporated.

Serves : 4-6

KADDU
(Dry Spicy Pumpkin)

1 kg pumpkin
  Green/yellow variety
  Red variety
100 gm oil (preferably
  mustard)
2 pieces of laung
1 tsp zeera
$^1/_4$ tsp methi dana
a pinch of hing

salt, lal mirch powder
  and hari mirch (finely
  chopped) to taste
$^1/_2$ tsp sonth powder
1 inch piece ginger
  (crushed)
1 tsp succh bari
  (powdered)

For the green/yellow variety, smoke oil and splutter the laung, zeera, methi dana and hing and put in the diced pumpkin. Shake the vessel a few times, add the rest of the spices and cover.

The red variety cooks better when peeled and cut into one and a half inch squares. The pieces are then put in oil and the vegetable tossed as usual. Very little water is needed. When the pumpkin is soft to touch, it is ready. Add haldi powder.

Variation : This vegetable may be prepared either by itself or with potatoes, fenugreek, radish or tomatoes.

Note : This vegetable is usually dry. As pumpkin releases water, keep the vessel on the fire for a long period so that all the liquid is absorbed.

Serves : 6-8

KARAMKALLA
(Dry Cabbage in Masala)

1 large cabbage
125 gm oil (preferably mustard)
a pinch of hing
1 tsp zeera
$1/2$ tsp methi dana
1 inch piece ginger (crushed)
2 hari mirch (finely chopped)
1 tsp sonth powder

salt and lal mirch powder to taste
1 tsp succh bari (powdered)
1 tsp sugar
1 tsp haldi powder (optional)
1 tsp dhania powder
a bunch of hara dhania leaves (finely chopped)

Cut the cabbage into four-inch pieces (do not shred). Smoke the oil, splutter the hing, zeera, methi dana, ginger, hari mirch and sonth. Add the cabbage, put in salt and lal mirch, succh bari, sugar and haldi, and shake the vessel till all the ingredients are well mixed. Put in two tablespoons of water and cook on a slow fire till soft but there should be no gravy left. Add dhania and toss again. Garnish with hara dhania.

Serves : 4-6

KABULI CHANA AND ALU
(Chick Peas with Potatoes)

250 gm chick peas
$^1/_4$ tsp sodium bicarbonate
200 gm oil (preferably
    mustard)
10 medium potatoes
2 onions (optional)
salt, lal mirch powder
    and hari mirch (finely
    chopped) to taste

$^1/_2$ tsp zeera
a pinch of hing
$^1/_2$ tsp sonth powder
1 inch piece ginger
    (crushed)
$^1/_2$ tsp garam masala
1 tsp dhania powder
a bunch of hara dhania
    leaves (finely chopped)

Soak the chick peas overnight, with the sodium bicarbonate. Next morning, wash with fresh water and boil it till soft.

Peel and cut the potatoes into fours. Heat the oil and fry the potatoes till light brown. Fry onions and add the boiled chick peas and masalas. Stir a couple of times and add a cup of water. Allow to simmer for fifteen minutes. When the water has evaporated, sprinkle over with hara dhania.

Serves : 8-10

KACHNAR
(Flowers of the Bauhinia Tree)

$^1/_2$ kg kachnar flowers
100 gm oil (preferably
    mustard)
$^1/_2$ tsp zeera
2 pieces of laung
salt, lal mirch powder
    and hari mirch (finely
    chopped) to taste

1 tsp dhania powder
1 tsp garam masala
$^1/_2$ tsp sonth powder
1 inch piece ginger
    (crushed)
a pinch of hing
a bunch of hara dhania
    leaves (finely chopped)

Boil the kachnar in water and when soft, strain, and remove the green outer stalk.

Heat oil and splutter the zeera, laung and hing. Add the kachnar and masalas, and fry till they turn reddish brown. Add half a cup of water and simmer for ten minutes. Whip the curd, and add it to the kachnar. Garnish with hara dhania. When ready, this vegetable should have a little gravy.

Serves : 4-6

KELE KE DAHI BARE
(Banana Kababs in Curd)

12 bananas (raw)
salt, lal mirch powder
  and hari mirch (finely
  chopped) to taste
2 tblsp breadcrumbs,
  arrowroot or cornflour
125 gm ghee or
  vegetable oil
250 gm curd

1 inch piece ginger
  (crushed)
1 tsp sonf (roasted and
  powdered)
1 tsp zeera (roasted and
  powdered)
a pinch of hing (roasted
  and powdered)
2 tsp dhania powder

Boil the bananas in their skins. Peel, mash and mix in salt, hari mirch and ginger. Mash again.

Add cornflour or breadcrumbs and mix thoroughly. Make into half-inch thick, oval kababs. Deep fry and set aside. When this is done, arrange the kababs on a plate and cover with cold, whipped curd. Sprinkle with a mixed spice made of sonf, zeera, roasted hing and dhania. Serve immediately.

Serves : 6-8

MEETHA KARELA
(Sweetened Bitter Gourd)

10 bitter gourds
1 tsp haldi
salt, lal mirch powder
    and hari mirch (finely
    chopped) to taste
$\frac{1}{2}$ tsp zeera (crushed)
2 tsp sonf (crushed)
$\frac{1}{2}$ tsp peppercorns
    (coarsely ground)
5-6 pieces of laung
    (ground)
10 tsp sugar
10 tsp amchur

10 medium onions
$\frac{1}{2}$ tsp kalonji
$\frac{1}{4}$ tsp methi dana
    (crushed)
2 inch piece ginger
    (crushed)
a bunch of pudina leaves
100 gm chana dal (soaked
    for thirty minutes)
100 gm oil (preferably
    mustard)
a pinch of hing

Scrape the outer skin of the bitter gourds and slit them lengthwise. Scoop out the seeds and pulp. Smear them inside-out with a mixture of haldi and salt and set aside, in a tilted position, to enable the bitter fluid to drain out. Let them remain in this position for half an hour.

Finely chop the onions. Mix in all the spices and salt to taste (except hing), sugar, amchur and pudina leaves. Add the dal to half this mixture. Drain out the remaining fluid in the bitter gourds by pressing them between your palms. Now stuff the bitter gourds with the onions, dal and masala mixture and either secure them with thread, or pierce with a toothpick, so that the slit does not open while cooking.

Take a vessel (preferably heavy-bottomed), heat the oil and splutter the hing. Place a layer of half the remaining onions at the bottom and then layer the stuffed bitter gourds, one by one, over them. Layer again with the remaining onions and bitter gourds, place the vessel on a slow fire and cover. (For best results, a few live charcoals should be placed on the lid of the vessel.) Cook for at least forty-five minutes. When the bitter gourds and dal are tender, remove the vessel from the fire.

Serves : 8-10

KHATTA KARELA
(Sour Bitter Gourd)

The ingredients are the same as for Dum Karela with the addition of :

2 tsp amchur **1 tsp haldi**
1 tsp sugar

Prepare as you would Dum Karela, but cut the bitter gourds into rounds, instead of lengthwise. When nearly done, add the sugar and amchur.

Note : Should you wish to use tomatoes, tamarind water or lemon juice, instead of amchur, the quantities are, one cup tomato juice, one tablespoon tamarind water and one tablespoon lemon juice. This dish is best made with mustard oil.

Serves : 10-12

BHARE KARELE
(Stuffed Bitter Gourd)

10 bitter gourds	$1/_2$ tsp kalonji
salt, lal mirch powder and hari mirch (finely chopped) to taste	2 tsp amchur powder
	$1/_2$ tsp methi dana
1 tsp haldi	1 tsp garam masala or succh bari (powdered)
5 medium potatoes	
2 medium onions (optional)	1 tsp zeera
	a pinch of hing
150 gm oil (preferably mustard)	1 tsp sonth powder
	1 inch piece ginger (crushed)
1 tsp dhania powder	1 tblsp pudina (chopped)
1 tsp sonf	

Scrape the outer skin of the bitter gourds and slit them lengthwise. Scoop out the seeds and pulp, and smear the bitter gourds with salt and haldi. After half an hour, press them between your palms to drain out the bitter fluid. Wash, peel and cut the potatoes into cubes, about one-eighth of an inch small. Dice the onions likewise.

Put the oil in a karhai and fry the potatoes and onions

in batches, till they turn light brown. Remove and set aside. Remove the karhai from the fire. Mix in all the ingredients with the fried potatoes and onions. Into this, mix in half the bitter gourd pulp that had been scooped out earlier. Mix all these ingredients thoroughly with your fingers. Now stuff the mixture into the bitter gourds and secure with a thread.

Place the karhai back on the fire and when the oil is hot, put in the bitter gourds (three or four at a time), and fry till they are uniformly brown. Remove them one by one. Take another vessel and put the remaining oil into it. Put all the bitter gourds and about two tablespoons of water into it and cook on a slow fire, for twenty minutes.

Variation : To make this into a non-vegetarian dish, substitute mince-meat, fried as in Dopyaza, for potatoes.

Serves : 8-10

BESAN KE KARELE
(Bitter Gourd in Gram Flour)

6 bitter gourds
60 gm oil (preferably
   mustard)
a pinch of hing
$1/_2$ tsp zeera
$1/_4$ tsp methi dana
$1/_2$ tsp sonf
$1/_4$ tsp kalonji
30 gm gram flour
$1/_2$ tsp sonth powder

salt, lal mirch powder
   and hari mirch (finely
   chopped) to taste
$1/_2$ inch piece ginger
   (crushed)
1 tsp dhania powder
a bunch of hara dhania
   or pudina leaves
   (finely chopped)

Scrape the bitter gourds and cut them into one-inch lengths. Heat the oil, splutter the hing, zeera, methi dana, sonf and kalonji. Add the bitter gourds and fry till they are light brown. Next, add the gram flour and fry till it turns light brown. Cover, till the moisture has almost evaporated. Now add the rest of the ingredients and mix with a ladle a few times. When the bitter gourds are tender, remove them from the fire and serve.

Serves : 4-6

PALAK
(Spiced Spinach)

½ kg spinach	¼ tsp methi dana
100 gm oil (preferably mustard)	15 gm fresh soya
a pinch of hing	1 tsp dhania powder
salt, lal mirch powder and hari mirch (finely chopped) to taste	1 tsp succh bari (powdered)
	1 tsp sonth powder
250 gm potatoes	1 tsp haldi powder
25 gm fresh fenugreek	1 inch piece ginger (crushed)
¼ tsp zeera	½ cup milk

Wash the spinach, discard the thick stems and chop the leaves finely.

Heat the oil, splutter the hing, zeera, methi dana and add the spinach. Cover. As the vegetable cooks, the water will evaporate. Now add the masalas and cook well, stirring with a ladle. Add milk and cook for some time till the vegetable acquires a thick consistency.

Variation : Should you prefer Palak Alu, fry the potatoes till light brown and add them to the spinach when it is nearly done. For Palak Methi or Palak Soya, add these vegetables to the spinach at the beginning of the cooking process.

Note : As this vegetable releases its own water do not add more. Milk added to any fried saag adds to its taste, especially spinach.

Serves : 4-6

PARWAL KI BHUJIA
(Dry Gherkins)

12 gherkins
100 gm ghee or
vegetable oil
a pinch of hing
$\frac{1}{2}$ tsp zeera
$\frac{1}{4}$ tsp methi dana
$\frac{1}{4}$ tsp kalonji

salt, lal mirch powder
and hari mirch (finely
chopped) to taste
1 tsp dhania powder
1 tsp haldi powder
$\frac{1}{2}$ tsp sonth powder

Scrape the gherkins, cut them lengthwise and then slice into half moons.

Heat the ghee, splutter the hing, zeera, methi dana, hari mirch and kalonji, and add the gherkins. Fry them for at least fifteen minutes, turning them over often. Cover and allow to simmer for another fifteen minutes. If the moisture has evaporated, add half a cup of water. Put in the remaining ingredients and another half cup of water. Cover and cook on a slow fire till the vegetable is soft and dry.

Serves : 4-6

BHARE PARWAL
(Stuffed Gherkins)

The ingredients are the same as for Bhare Karele, except that twelve large gherkins are used instead of bitter gourds.

Scrape the gherkins, slit lengthwise and scoop out the pulp. Then follow the same method as for Bhare Karele.

Serves : 8-10

PARWAL RASDAAR
(Spiced Gherkins in Gravy)

The ingredients are the same as for Parwal ki Bhujia, with the addition of :

1 tsp haldi powder   1 tsp flour

Slit the gherkins as you would for Dum Parwal and cook in the same manner, adding haldi as well. As this dish requires some gravy, it should be thickened with one teaspoon of flour, which is added a few minutes before the vegetable is done.

Serves : 4-6

PHOOL GOBHI
(Cauliflower in Masala)

1 large or 2 small
   cauliflowers
125 gm oil (preferably
   mustard)
a pinch of hing
1 tsp zeera
1 inch piece ginger
   (crushed)
1 tsp sonth powder
1 tsp succh bari
   (powdered)

$^1/_2$ tsp methi dana
1 tsp sugar
salt, lal mirch powder
   and hari mirch (finely
   chopped) to taste
1 tsp haldi powder
   (optional)
1 tsp dhania powder
a bunch of hara dhania
   leaves (finely chopped)

Cut the cauliflower into two-inch florets. Heat the oil, sprinkle a little water and splutter the hing, zeera, methi dana, ginger, hari mirch, sonth and fry for a few seconds. Add the cauliflower, put in the salt, lal mirch, succh bari, sugar, haldi and shake the vessel, so that the masala is well mixed. Put in two tablespoons of water and cook on a slow fire till the stems get soft (put in more water if necessary). Add dhania and toss again. Finally, garnish with hara dhania.

Serves : 4-6

RAZMAH
(Kidney Beans Curry)

250 gm razmah
$1/2$ tsp sodium bicarbonate
100 gm ghee or
    vegetable oil
a pinch of hing
$1/2$ tsp zeera
$1/2$ tsp sonth powder
100 gm curd
$1/2$ tsp garam masala

1 inch piece ginger
   (crushed)
salt, lal mirch powder
   and hari mirch (finely
   chopped) to taste
1 tsp dhania powder
a bunch of hara dhania
   leaves (finely chopped)

Soak razmah overnight with the sodium bicarbonate. Next morning drain, and boil in fresh water in a pressure cooker. When soft, drain and set aside. Heat the ghee and splutter the hing, zeera, sonth, curd and ginger. When the curd turns light brown, add salt, lal and hari mirch and the razmah. Fry for five or ten minutes. Add half a cup of water and allow to simmer for ten minutes. Then add garam masala, dhania and hara dhania. Cover and cook till done.

Serves : 4-6

RASDAAR PAKORI
(Gram Flour/Lentil Dumplings in Gravy)

250 gm gram flour, or
moong dal (dhuli or
chilka), or red
masoor, or chana, or
a mixture of any two
dals
250 gm oil (preferably
mustard)
1 tsp haldi powder

salt and lal mirch
powder to taste
1 tsp dhania powder
$1/2$ tsp sonth powder
1 tsp garam masala
1 tblsp ghee
$1/2$ tsp zeera
a pinch of hing

If using gram flour, test the batter as explained earlier
(see recipe for Kabargah). Put the oil in a karhai, and
when hot, drop in small lumps of batter for pakoris.
Remove and set aside. Boil two cups of water. Add
haldi, salt, lal mirch, dhania and sonth. Now put in the
pakoris and simmer for ten minutes. As soon as the
pakoris swell and are soft to touch, add garam masala.
Take a tablespoon of hot ghee, add zeera and hing,
and pour over the pakoris.

If using dal, soak whichever you are using in water for
a few hours. Drain, and grind to a thick, smooth paste.
Beat well and test the batter as before. Make pakoris
but save two or three tablespoons of the batter. In a
separate vessel, put in this batter with three cups of
water, and the masalas, except garam masala, zeera
and hing. Boil for about five minutes. Add the pakoris.
When they swell and become soft, add the garam
masala. Take a tablespoon of hot ghee, add zeera
and hing, and pour over the pakoris.

Serves : 4-6

HAAK
(Kashmiri Spinach)

$^1/_2$ kg haak	$^1/_4$ tsp zeera
10 gm oil (preferably mustard)	$^1/_4$ tsp methi dana
	1 tsp dhania powder
a pinch of hing	1 tsp succh bari (powdered)
salt, lal mirch powder and hari mirch (finely chopped) to taste	1 tsp sonth powder
	1 tsp haldi powder
1 tsp sugar or $^1/_2$ inch gur	$^1/_2$ inch piece ginger (crushed)

This is a leafy saag grown mainly in Kashmir but can also be grown in the plains during winter. It resembles the tender leaves of a cauliflower. This saag is cooked whole, not cut like the others. The method is as follows: Heat the oil, add hing and all the masalas. Fry for a second. Boil two cups of water and add the haak. Allow to simmer for twenty minutes. When it softens, add gur or sugar and remove from the fire after a few minutes. Make sure a little gravy remains. Haak is served with rice.

Serves : 4-6

KARAM HAAK

This is a leafy saag with a bulbous root. While haak leaves are cooked whole, karam haak leaves are cut into two or three pieces. The ingredients and method are the same as for Haak. However, the root should be shallow-fried in oil with salt and lal mirch powder and added to the saag.

DIVANI HANDIA
(Mixed Vegetables)

4 brinjals (500 gm)
125 gm spinach
30 gm fenugreek
1 radish
1 onion
25 gm soya
100 gm oil (preferably mustard)
a pinch of hing
$1/_2$ tsp zeera
$1/_4$ tsp methi dana
$1/_2$ cup milk

salt, lal mirch powder and hari mirch (finely chopped) to taste
1 tsp haldi powder
1 tsp dhania powder
1 tsp succh bari (powdered)
1 tsp sonth powder
1 inch piece ginger (crushed)
a bunch of hara dhania leaves (finely chopped)

Finely chop all the vegetables. Heat the oil, and splutter the hing, zeera and methi dana. Immediately add the vegetables. Cover and cook till the liquid from the vegetables evaporates. With a ladle keep stirring the vegetables so that they fry well. Add milk and the remaining masalas. Fry a little longer, till the milk is absorbed by the vegetables and oil appears on the surface. Remove, and garnish with hara dhania.

Serves : 4-6

SAAG
(Leafy Vegetable)

Sarson, Karam Haak, Nari, Chana, Bathua, Cholai

The ingredients are the same as for Palak

Wash, clean and finely chop whichever saag you choose. Cook the saag as you would Palak

Note : If chane ka saag is used, cut and boil the leaves first for ten minutes, because they are not as tender as those of the other varieties.

Serves : 4-6

TAMATAR AUR HARA DHANIA
(Tomatoes and Coriander)

1 kg tomatoes
100 gm hara dhania
4 medium onions
100 gm ghee or vegetable oil
a pinch of hing
1 tsp zeera

salt, lal mirch powder and hari mirch (finely chopped) to taste
1 inch piece ginger (crushed)
1 tsp dhania powder
2 tsp sugar

Cut the tomatoes into small pieces, and finely chop the hara dhania and onions. Heat the ghee, add the onions and fry them lightly. Now splutter the hing, zeera and tomatoes and cook for ten to fifteen minutes. Then add the remaining masalas and when the vegetable thickens, sprinkle over the hara dhania and sugar. Remove from fire.

Note : Not only is this dish served as a vegetable, it can also be used as a paste or spread.

Serves : 8-10

TAO GUGJI / SHALJAM
(Dry Spiced Turnips)

1 kg turnips
150 gm ghee or
  vegetable oil
1 tsp zeera
a pinch of hing
4 pieces of laung
2 hari mirch (finely
  chopped)
1 inch piece ginger
  (crushed)

salt and lal mirch
  powder to taste
1 tsp haldi powder
1 tsp sugar
1 tsp sonth powder
2 tsp dhania powder
1 tsp garam masala or
  succh bari (powdered)
a bunch of hara dhania
  leaves (finely chopped)

Peel and cut the turnips into fours. Lightly fry them in ghee, and set aside. Heat the ghee and splutter the zeera, hing, laung, hari mirch, ginger and sonth. Add the turnips, salt, lal mirch, haldi, sugar, and pour in one and a half cups of water. Simmer on low heat for about ten minutes, then add dhania and garam masala and simmer till the water evaporates. Garnish with hara dhania.

Serves : 6-8

BHARE TINDE
(Stuffed Gourd)

1 kg gourds
6 medium potatoes (cut
　into 1 inch cubes)
2 onions (chopped)
125 gm ghee or
　vegetable oil
salt, lal mirch powder
　and hari mirch (finely
　chopped) to taste
2 tsp amchur powder
1 tsp dhania powder
1 tsp zeera

$1/_2$ tsp kalonji
1 tsp haldi powder
$1/_4$ tsp methi dana
1 tsp sonth powder
a pinch of hing
1 inch piece ginger
　(crushed)
1 tsp garam masala
toothpicks
a bunch of hara dhania
　leaves (finely chopped)

Wash and scrape the gourds and cut off half an inch from the top to make a lid. Scoop out the pulp and set the gourds aside.

Fry the potatoes till light brown and set aside. Then fry the onions till brown and mix in the fried potatoes. Add the salt, all the masalas and the hara dhania. Stuff the mixture into the gourds and cover with the lids. Insert a toothpick into each gourd to secure the lid. (Thread may be used instead, but it must be wound carefully as it often slips off the round gourds.)

Heat the oil in a frying pan. When hot, place the gourds in it, two or three at a time. Gently turn them around till they turn light brown. Set aside, as they get done. Put the remaining oil in another vessel and heat. Put in the fried gourds, add a little water and cover. Allow to simmer for fifteen minutes, till they are soft. Remove and serve.

Serves : 8-10

BHAZBHATTA / TEHRI
(Vegetable Pulao)

¹/₂ kg rice
200 gm ghee or
    vegetable oil
a pinch of hing
1 tsp zeera
250 gm potatoes (cut in
    fours)
1 medium cauliflower
250 gm peas (shelled)
salt, lal mirch powder
    and hari mirch (finely
    chopped) to taste

4 tejpattas
4 pieces of laung
1 tsp garam masala
1 tsp haldi powder
    (optional)
2 tsp dhania powder
1 tsp succh bari
2 tomatoes (optional)
2 onions (finely sliced
    and fried; optional)
a bunch of hara dhania
    leaves (finely chopped)

Soak rice in water for an hour. Heat ghee, splutter the hing, zeera and laung. Add the soaked rice and fry for three or four minutes. Fry the potatoes in a separate karhai. Add the potatoes, cauliflower and peas to the rice, then put in the tejpatta, masalas, tomatoes and fried onions. Pour water (one and a quarter times the weight of the rice) and allow to simmer for fifteen minutes. Sprinkle the chopped hara dhania and check to see whether the rice has absorbed the water and is cooked. Add a little more water, if insufficient. For best results, place the vessel on a charcoal fire with some live coals on the lid. If you are using gas, place a tava on the flame and put the covered vessel on it.

Variation : In this method, first the vegetables are added to the ghee together with the hing, zeera and laung and fried for a few minutes. Then rice is added and fried again for a few minutes. Finally water and the rest of the ingredients are added and cooked as above.

Serves : 4-6

TURAI
(Snake Gourd)

1 kg snake gourd
100 gm ghee or
   vegetable oil
$1/_2$ tsp zeera
a pinch of hing
2 pieces of laung
salt, lal mirch powder
   and hari mirch (finely
   chopped) to taste
$1/_4$ tsp methi dana

1 tsp dhania powder
1 tsp succh or petha
   bari (powdered)
1 tsp haldi powder
$1/_2$ tsp sonth powder
1 inch piece ginger
   (crushed)
a bunch of hara dhania
   leaves (finely chopped)

Peel and cut the snake gourd into rounds, half an inch thick. Heat the oil, and splutter the zeera, methi dana, hing and laung. After a few seconds add the snake gourd. Cover and allow to simmer for fifteen to twenty minutes. (As snake gourd releases its own water, do not add any more.) Move the vegetable once or twice, then add salt and the rest of the masalas. Cook till the oil appears on the surface, and all the water evaporates. Garnish with chopped hara dhania.

Variation : Should you wish to add potatoes to the vegetables, fry them first and put them in with the masalas.

Note : For a better flavour, a teaspoon of petha bari, powdered, may be added with the spices.

Serves : 6-8

TAMATAR MULI
(Spicy Tomatoes and Radish)

6 large tomatoes
2 radish
100 gm oil (preferably
   mustard)
$\frac{1}{2}$ tsp zeera
a pinch of hing
salt, lal mirch powder
   and hari mirch (finely
   chopped) to taste
$\frac{1}{4}$ tsp methi dana

1 tsp sugar
1 tsp succh bari
   (powdered)
1 tsp sonth powder
1 tsp dhania powder
1 inch piece ginger
   (crushed)
a bunch of hara dhania
   leaves (finely chopped)

Wash and cut tomatoes finely. Wash and scrape the radish and cut them into rounds, half-inch wide.

Heat the oil and splutter the zeera, hing and methi dana. Now add the tomatoes. When they are half done, add the radish, sugar and the rest of the masalas. Cover till the radish becomes soft. (Add a little water if necessary.) Garnish with hara dhania.

Serves : 4-6

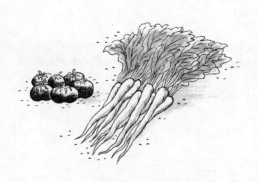

CHAVAL
(Plain Rice)

$1/_2$ kg rice

Wash the rice in water, rubbing the grains gently with your palms, and allow it to soak for at least one hour. In another vessel, put water, at least twice the weight of the rice, and bring it to a boil. Drain the water from the soaked rice and add the rice to the boiling water. Stir the rice occasionally with a perforated ladle. As the rice boils it gradually increases in size. Be careful not to allow it to overboil and become too soft.

Pick up a few grains of rice with the ladle and rub between thumb and forefinger to see whether it is cooked—it should still be slightly hard, however. Add cold water, about two cups, stir lightly once and drain all the water out after covering the vessel with a lid. (Place the vessel on a charcoal fire and put a few live charcoals on the lid. This process will give the best results.) To test if the rice is done, remove the lid and place the back of your hand over the rice. If the rice is ready, a few grains will automatically stick to your fingers.

Should you be cooking on gas, after draining the water from the cooked rice, place a tava on the flame and put the vessel over it for a few minutes, till the rice is done.

Serves : 4-6

ARHAR KI DAL
(Yellow Lentils)

All dals may be cooked in two different ways, liquid or dry. Dal can either be plain or sour.

250 gm dal	1 inch piece gur
a pinch of hing	25 to 50 gm desi ghee
1 tsp haldi powder	2 pieces of laung
salt to taste	

Liquid Dal : Soak dal in water for an hour. In a round, heavy-bottomed vessel, put in the soaked dal and enough fresh water to cover the dal only. Add half the hing, haldi and salt. Cover and allow to boil. When the water has almost evaporated and the dal shows signs of softening, add half a cup of water, cover again and leave on a slow fire till it is soft to touch. Let all the water evaporate and, when the dal is quite dry, turn it with a ladle in a circular motion for about five minutes. This process will turn the dal into a soft pulp. Now gradually pour in half a cup of hot water and mix thoroughly to thin the dal. To make it tastier, add some fresh, hot, strained, boiled rice water. Stir the dal and rice water slowly to arrive at a fairly thick consistency. Add gur and cook for another five minutes on a slow fire. (To give the dal a smoother consistency, sieve it so that all uncooked grains are removed.)

Heat ghee in a frying pan and splutter the laung and the rest of the hing and pour them over the dal. (A common variation is to add turnips, cut in fours, and cooked with the dal. Take care to remove the turnips from the dal before turning it with a ladle. Put them back again after this is done.)

Dry Dal : Follow the same process as for liquid dal. When the dal softens and splits, remove it from the fire. Add powdered gur and hot ghee with hing and laung.

Alternatively, first heat the ghee, splutter the hing and laung and immediately add the strained, soaked dal. Fry for a few minutes. Now add salt and haldi and enough water to cover the dal.. Cook on a slow fire till the dal is soft to touch. Put in the powdered gur, and add more water in small quantities, as required, till the dal is quite soft, yet dry.

Variation : To make sour Dal, add amchur, tomato pulp or lemon juice, according to taste.

Serves : 6-8

FOR COOKS SHORT-ON-TIME

Liquid Dal : Soak dal in water for an hour. Drain the water from the dal and put it into a pressure cooker, add half the hing, haldi, gur, salt and enough fresh water to cover the dal. Pressurize for five minutes. The water will have evaporated and the dal will now be a soft pulp. Pour a cup of water or a little more and mix thoroughly to thin the dal.

Heat ghee in a frying pan, splutter the laung and the rest of the hing and pour them over the dal.

Dry Dal : Follow the same process as for liquid dal. When the dal softens and splits, remove it from the fire. Add powdered gur. Season with hot ghee, hing and laung.

CHANE KI DAL
(Yellow Split Lentils)

250 gm dal
salt to taste
1 tsp haldi powder
$\frac{1}{2}$ tsp zeera
1 inch piece ginger
    (crushed)
$\frac{1}{2}$ tsp sonth powder
25-50 gm desi ghee

1 onion (chopped;
    optional)
1 tsp sonf
2 pieces of laung
a pinch of hing
25 gm pudina (fresh or
    dried)

Liquid Dal : Follow the same process as for Arhar ki Dal, but the ladle or karchi must be sparingly used so that the soft grains of the dal do not break. When the water has almost evaporated and the grains are soft, add the masalas, except onions, sonf, laung and ghee. Pour in a cup of hot water and another cup of hot, strained, rice water and cook for a few minutes. Heat the ghee, fry the onions to a reddish brown and add sonf, laung and hing. Pour this over the dal and sprinkle over with pudina.

Tomatoes, cut in fours, may be added if desired. Also add a little sugar or gur. Bottle gourd, brinjal and pumpkin can be substituted for a change; boil and soften them with the dal.

Dry Dal : Follow the recipe for Arhar ki Dal, but no water or rice water should be added after the dal has softened.

Serves 6-8

MASOOR KI DAL
(Red / Black Lentils)

250 gm dal
a pinch of hing
1 tsp haldi powder
salt and lal mirch
   powder to taste
1 tsp dhania powder
$\frac{1}{2}$ tsp zeera

1 inch piece ginger
   (crushed)
25-50 gm desi ghee
2 pieces of laung
25 gm pudina (fresh or
   dried)

Red : Soak dal in water for an hour. In a round, heavy-bottomed vessel, put in the soaked dal and enough fresh water to cover the dal only. Add half the hing, haldi and salt. Cover and allow to boil. When the water has almost evaporated and the dal shows signs of softening, add half a cup of water, cover again and leave on a slow fire till it is soft to touch. Let all the water evaporate and when the dal is almost dry, turn it with a ladle, in a circular motion, for about five minutes. Add the masalas except zeera, hing, laung, and ghee. Pour in a cup of hot water and another cup of hot, strained rice water. Make sure the water is hot or lumps will form in the dal. While cooking, stir slowly to arrive at a fairly thick consistency. Heat the ghee and add hing, zeera and laung. When hot, pour over the dal.

Black : Follow the same process as for Arhar ki Dal, except that when the dal has softened, stir it lightly with a ladle so that the soft grains do not break and the dal attains a thick consistency. Add the lal mirch, ginger and dhania now. Pour half a cup of hot water and allow to simmer for about five minutes. In a separate vessel heat ghee, zeera, laung and hing. When hot, pour over the dal and sprinkle over with pudina.

Variation : This variety of dal is usually made sour by adding either amchur or lemon or tomato juice to taste. This should be done five minutes before it is ready to remove from heat.

Serves 6-8

MOONG KI DAL—DHULI
(Yellow Lentils)

250 gm dal
salt to taste
1 tsp haldi powder
1 inch piece ginger
  (ground)
1 cup milk

1 inch piece gur
  (crushed)
25-50 gm desi ghee
a pinch of hing
2 pieces of laung
$1/_2$ tsp zeera

Liquid Dal : Follow the same process as for Arhar ki Dal, except that when you add the boiled, strained rice water, or water or milk, they must be hot or else lumps will form in the dal. Add milk abut ten minutes before the dal is ready. Also, zeera is added to the ghee together with the laung and hing.

For variety, add boiled Bathua Saag.

Dry Dal : Follow the same process as for Arhar ki Dal, except that zeera is also added to the hot ghee together with hing and laung.

For sour Moong ki Dal, follow the same process as for sour Arhar. However, no milk should be added, as it will curdle.

Serves 6-8

MOONG KI DAL—CHILKA
(Split Lentils)

250 gm dal
salt to taste
$^1/_4$ tsp lal mirch powder
1 tsp dhania powder
$^1/_2$ tsp sonth powder
1 tsp haldi powder
1 inch piece gur

1 inch piece ginger
  (ground)
25-50 gm desi ghee
a pinch of hing
$^1/_2$ tsp zeera
2 pieces of laung

Liquid Dal : Wash the dal and soak it for an hour and a half. Remove half the skin by gently rubbing the grains with your palms. To the remaining dal add enough water to cover. Add masalas and bring it to a boil.

Now follow the same process as for Arhar ki Dal.

For variety, add muli or turnips, cut into rounds and boiled till soft. Bathua Saag may also be used.

Dry Dal : Follow the same process as for Arhar ki Dal (dry), except that zeera is also added to the hot ghee together with hing and laung.

Serves 6-8

DAL—KAYOTI
(Mixed Lentils)

125 gm chana dal   125 gm urad dal (dhuli)

The rest of the ingredients are the same as for Chane ki Dal. Follow the same process as for Chane ki Dal.

Serves 4-6

DAL—PACHMEL
(Mixture of Five Lentils)

Five dals are used together in this recipe.

50 gm arhar dal   **50 gm moong dal (dhuli)**
50 gm chana dal   **50 gm moong dal (chilka)**
50 gm urad dal (dhuli)

The rest of the masalas and ghee are the same as for Moong (Chilka). Follow the same process also as for Moong (Chilka).

Serves 6-8

URAD KI DAL—DHULI AND CHILKA
(Black Lentils—Washed and Split)

250 gm dal   **1 tsp sonf**
salt and lal mirch   **1 inch piece ginger**
powder to taste   **(crushed)**
$\frac{1}{2}$ tsp sonth powder   **1 onion (shredded and**
1 tsp haldi powder   **fried; optional)**
(optional)   **25-50 gm desi ghee**
1 tsp dhania powder   **a pinch of hing**

Liquid Dal : Follow the same process as for Chane ki Dal.

Dry Dal : Follow the same process as for Chane ki Dal.

Serves 6-8

MOONG KI DAL—SABUT
(Whole Green Lentils)

250 gm dal
salt and lal mirch
   powder to taste
$\frac{1}{2}$ tsp sonth powder
1 tsp haldi powder
$\frac{1}{2}$ tsp zeera

1 inch piece ginger
   (crushed)
25-50 gm desi ghee
a pinch of hing
2 pieces of laung

Follow the same process as for Moong ki dal (Chilka), but do not remove the chilka.

Serves 6-8

DRIED / DEHYDRATED VEGETABLES

The ingredients are the same as for any plain, fresh vegetable recipe.

All dried vegetables, except tomatoes, should be soaked overnight with a little sodium bicarbonate. This almost doubles their size. Wash the vegetables, and use fresh water to boil them till tender. Strain and cook, as you would fresh vegetables. Tomatoes should not be boiled, but added to the vegetable a few minutes before it is done. In the case of dried cauliflower, add curd towards the end of the cooking process.

Note : See pages xxiii-xxv for instructions on how to prepare dried vegetables.

PULAO
(Aromatic Rice)

$^1/_2$ kg rice
3 pieces of laung
5-6 choti elaichis
1 tsp garam masala
4 tejpattas
100 gm desi ghee
25 gm kishmish

25 gm badam (shelled, soaked and skinned)
$^1/_2$ tsp shah zeera
a pinch of zafran
1 tsp keora water
$^1/_2$ cup milk

Wash and soak the rice for an hour. In a separate vessel put in two and a half litres of water. In a small muslin bag, tie in the laung, choti elaichi, garam masala and tejpatta and place it in the water. Boil for half an hour. When the colour of the water resembles light tea, drain the soaked rice and add it to the spiced water. Stir the rice gently once in a while till it is three-quarters done. Cover the vessel with a lid, drain the water, and set aside.

Heat the ghee in a small saucepan or frying pan and when hot, add the kishmish and badam. When the kishmish swells, remove from fire, and pour the ghee, kishmish and badam over the rice. Mix well, with the handle of a ladle. Add shah zeera and repeat the process. Grind the zafran in keora water and sprinkle it over the rice. Pour the milk around the rice and cover the vessel. Now place it over a charcoal fire and put some live coals on the lid. Let it remain thus for fifteen to twenty minutes. Then remove the vessel from the fire.

Variation : Should you prefer to have a multi-coloured pulao, put in a few drops of green and red edible colour and mix it in lightly with the handle of the ladle.

Serves : 4-6

MOTI OR CHAMAN PULAO
(Pearl Pulao with Peas and Cottage Cheese)

The ingredients are the same as for Pulao, with the addition of :

250 gm chaman   **2 tblsp sugar**
250 gm peas   **4 silver leaves**

For Chaman Pulao : Prepare the pulao according to the recipe for Pulao.

Cut the chaman into slices and then into cubes of half-inch thickness. Fry lightly in ghee and set aside. In a vessel put in the sugar and one tablespoon water and make into a very thick syrup. Add the fried chaman to the pulao and mix with the syrup.

For Moti Pulao : Boil the peas, strain, and add them to the syrup. Place the vessel on a fire and turn the peas till they are fully coated with the syrup and are almost dry. Put the silver leaves on the peas and remove the vessel from the fire. Roll the vessel continuously till all the peas are coated with silver leaf and resemble little silver balls.

Note : For Moti Pulao, add the silver-coated peas to the cooked pulao a few minutes before serving.

Serves : 4-6

SARVARI
(Rice with Black Gram, Chick Peas or Peas)

150 gm rice
100 gm chick peas,
    black gram or peas
    (shelled)
$1/2$ tsp sodium bicarbonate

1 tsp salt
50 gm desi ghee
1 tsp zeera
2 pieces of laung

If you are using chick peas or black gram, soak overnight in water with the sodium bicarbonate. Next morning, wash the chick peas/black gram in fresh water, boil till soft, and strain. Set aside. If you use peas, boil them till tender, strain and set aside.

Wash and soak the rice in water for an hour. Cook it as you would plain rice. When done, turn the cooked rice on to a thali and sprinkle over with salt. Heat the ghee, splutter the zeera and laung and pour the ghee over the rice. Now add either the chick peas, black gram or peas, and mix well with a ladle, being careful not to break the rice. Turn it back into the vessel and cover, placing a few live charcoals over the lid.

Note : In Kashmiri Pandit homes, Sarvari is cooked on auspicious occasions, like birthdays, Nauroz, etc.

Serves : 4-6

GUCHCHI
(Spicy Dehydrated Mushrooms)

200 gm mushrooms
  (dehydrated)
100 gm ghee or
  vegetable oil
$1/_2$ tsp sonth powder
3 pieces of laung
salt and hari mirch
  (finely chopped)
  to taste
a pinch of hing

$1/_2$ tsp zeera
$1/_2$ tsp lal mirch powder
1 tsp garam masala
1 tsp dhania powder
1 inch piece ginger
  (crushed)
50 gm curd (whipped)
a bunch of hara dhania
  leaves (finely chopped)

Soak the mushrooms in three to four cups of water for about two hours. Remove and boil in fresh water till tender. Strain and set aside. Heat the ghee, splutter the sonth, laung, hing and zeera. Add the boiled mushrooms and fry for about five minutes. Put in a quarter-cup water, add the salt, lal and hari mirch, garam masala, dhania, ginger and finally the whipped curd. When the water has very nearly evaporated, the dish is ready. Garnish with hara dhania.

Variation : This vegetable can also be cooked in syrup and made into a sweet dish. No masala is needed, but keora water is used for flavouring. The mushrooms are first boiled and then simmered in a thin syrup.

Serves : 6-8

BARIAN
(Creamy Spiced Rice with Almonds)

250 gm rice
2 tsp salt
1/2 tsp lal mirch powder
hari mirch (finely
    chopped) to taste
1 tsp sonth powder
1 tsp dhania powder
1 tsp garam masala
a pinch of hing

1 tsp succh bari
    (powdered)
50 gm desi ghee
1 tsp zeera
3 pieces of laung
15 badams (shelled,
    soaked, skinned
    and cut in two)

Wash and soak the rice in water for an hour. In a degchi put in four cups of water and bring it to a boil. Add the strained rice. When the grains soften, turn the ladle in a rotary motion, so that the grains are well crushed and the mixture turns into a pulp. Keep stirring constantly so that it does not stick and burn. If the consistency is too thick, add a little more water so that the mixture acquires a thick, syrupy appearance. When this is done, add all the masalas except for zeera, hing, laung and badam.

Add another two cups of water and allow to simmer for ten minutes till the mixture becomes a thick paste.

Heat the ghee in the frying pan, splutter the zeera, laung, badam and hing and pour it over the cooked barian.

Note : Fried guchchis added while cooking improves the taste of this dish. This traditional Kashmiri Pandit dish is prepared at the beginning of weddings, which initiates the festivities.

Serves : 6-8

ALU OR ARVI KI KURKURI
(Fine Potato / Yam Fries)

125 gm potatoes (large),
or
125 gm yam (long)
200 gm oil (preferably
  mustard)

$^1/_4$ tsp sodium bicarbonate
salt and lal mirch
  powder to taste
a pinch of hing (roasted
  and powdered)

Wash and peel the potatoes or yam, cut them into fine finger chips, lengthwise, and soak them in salt water (with the sodium bicarbonate) for fifteen minutes. Drain and spread them on a piece of cloth so that the moisture is absorbed.

Heat oil in a karhai and when quite hot, fry these chips, two tablespoonfuls, at a time, till golden brown and crisp. Remove and spread on a sheet of paper in a small bamboo basket. (The paper and bamboo will absorb the surplus oil.) When all the kurkuris (chips) are done, sprinkle over with salt, lal mirch and hing. Toss the kurkuris to mix. Keep in a warm place so that they retain their crispness. (Do not cover as this tends to make them soft.)

Note : A gadget for making potato fingers and chips may be used.

Serves : 6-8

RAITA
(Mixed Vegetable Curd)

With any one of the following vegetables : potatoes, brinjal, okra, spinach, radish, onions or cucumber or boondi

$1/_2$ kg curd
125 gm potatoes
or 250 gm okra
or 125 gm brinjal
or 125 gm spinach
or 3 medium radish
or 4 medium onions
or 2 medium cucumber
or 125 gm boondi
$1/_2$ tsp mustard (powdered)
1 tsp dhania powder

$1/_2$ tsp zeera (roasted and powdered)
$1/_2$ tsp sonf (roasted and powdered)
a pinch of hing (roasted and powdered)
salt, lal mirch powder and hari mirch (finely chopped) to taste
a bunch of hara dhania leaves (finely chopped)

Whip the curd to a creamy consistency and then add any of the following vegetables, together with the masalas and hara dhania.

Potatoes : Boil, peel and cut finely or crush with the fingers. Add to the curd.

Okra : Wash and cut into thin slices and fry lightly in very little ghee on a tava or in a frying pan. When cool, add to the curd.

Brinjal : Either roast or steam it whole. When it is soft, squeeze out the pulp and throw away the skin. Mix into the curd.

Spinach : Wash and nip the leaves only. Chop finely and fry lightly. Mix in with the curd.

Radish : Wash, scrape and grate. Mix into the curd.

Onions : Peel and grate, and mix as above.

Cucumber : Treat the same way as radish, but press the liquid out of the grated cucumber before putting it into the curd. For a better taste, add a teaspoon of sugar to the curd. Garnish with hara dhania.

Boondi : Either buy ready-made boondi or make it at home in the following manner: Prepare a batter of gram flour and test it for the correct consistency (as in the recipe for Kabargah). Heat oil in a vessel, and pour the prepared batter through a perforated ladle by striking the stem of the ladle against the edge of the vessel. Remove the boondi with another ladle as soon as it begins to swell. Any delay in doing so might result in their being overcooked and becoming dark. Set aside till cool. Mix in with the curd.

Raita is served cold.

Serves : 6-8

KARHI
(Dumplings in Gram Flour Gravy)

250 gm gram flour
200 gm oil
salt and lal mirch
  powder to taste
1 tsp haldi powder
1 tsp dhania powder
$^1/_2$ tsp sonth powder
125 gm curd

1 tblsp lemon juice
50 gm desi ghee
$^1/_2$ tsp zeera
a pinch of hing
a bunch of hara dhania
  or pudina leaves
  (finely chopped)

Make a batter with gram flour and water and beat. (To test the batter drop a lump into a cup of water—it should float.) Pour the oil into a karhai, and make boondis (about half-an-inch in diameter; see method for boondis under Raita), reserving about two tablespoons of the batter for the gravy.

In another vessel, put in the remaining batter, thinned with some water, add another four to five cups of water and bring it to a boil. Cook, stirring continuously, till the raw smell of the gram flour disappears. Add salt, lal mirch, haldi, dhania and sonth and allow to simmer for another two to three minutes. Add the fried boondis and simmer again for five minutes. Meanwhile, whip the curd, and add it and the lemon juice to the boondis. Simmer for another few minutes. When the karhi is ready, heat the desi ghee, splutter the zeera and hing and pour it into the karhi. Sprinkle with hara dhania or pudina leaves.

Variation : A variation of karhi is made by using pakoris instead of boondis.

Serves : 8-10

BREADS

PHULKA / CHAPATTI
(Hot Fluffed Bread)

$^1/_2$ kg wheat flour   water to mix

Sieve the wheat flour onto a thali, set aside a cupful, and mix the rest with enough water to make a soft dough. Knead well, cover with another thali and set aside for at least half an hour. Now place a tava on the fire and as it warms up, make fifteen balls of the dough. Flatten them and press each into the flour, which has been kept aside. Using a rolling pin, roll into rounds on a chakla till they are eight to nine inches across in width, being careful to make the edges thinner than the centre. Lift the phulka off the chakla and place it on the hot tava. As it dries, turn the phulka onto the other side, using a chumta. Wait a few seconds, lifting it with the chumta now and then to see if black specks have appeared. Remove the tava. Finally, put the phulka onto the open flame or fire, on the top side. Turn the phulka once more on the open flame. It should puff up into a round ball. The phulka is now ready to serve.

Serves : 6-8

PAHRATHI / PARATHA
(Hot Layered Bread)

$^1/_2$ kg wheat flour   200 gm ghee or
water to mix   vegetable oil

Sieve the wheat flour onto a thali. Set aside a cupful and mix the rest with enough water to make a dough (this should be slightly stiffer than that made for phulkas).

Knead well, cover with another thali and set aside for half an hour. Make balls of the dough and roll them on a chakla (like phulkas, but they should be slightly thicker). Now smear a little ghee with a spoon onto the chapatti, fold it over in half, smear some more ghee on it and fold it in half again. Roll into a triangular shape, making the edges thinner than the centre. Place on a hot tava, turn over once and smear with ghee again. Cook for a few seconds, turn over again and smear the other side with ghee as well. Cook for another few seconds till the pahrathi is golden brown on both sides.

Alternatively, make the dough as above, rolling out into eight-inch rounds. Smear with ghee, and with one hand roll it into a round stick. Now with a rolling pin flatten it to a two-inch width. Smear ghee on it and fold one-third. Next, fold the remaining one-third over the first fold, roll out again into a rectangular shape, and cook as above.

Serves : 4-6

SIR PITTI PHULKI
(Ghee-smeared Flat Bread)

100 gm ghee or   **½ kg whole wheat flour**
vegetable oil

Cook like chapattis, but when black specks form on the phulka, smear ghee on both sides and turn over twice on the tava. Do not place them on an open fire. Make sure that both sides develop black specks before you apply ghee.

Serves : 6-8

KHAMEERI ROTI
(Sweetened Yeast Bread)

$1/2$ kg wheat flour	$1/2$ cup milk (approx)
$1/2$ tsp salt	2-3 tblsp sugar
1 tblsp sonf (powdered)	50 gm ghee (desi)
2 tblsp khameer	

Mix together the wheat flour, salt, sonf and khameer. Sweeten the milk with sugar and add it to the mixture. Knead into a soft dough for about fifteen minutes. Set aside. After a few hours, knead it again to allow it to rise. Keep it in a covered vessel in a warm place till it rises to twice its original size. Using the dough, make thick rotis, five to six inches in diameter. Roll them as you would phulkas. Bake them over an open fire.

Before serving, smear desi ghee on each hot roti.

Serves : 10-12

MAZ PHASHI ROTI
(Ghee-layered Puffed Bread)

100 gm ghee or vegetable oil	$1/2$ **kg whole wheat flour**

Make dough as you would for chapattis and smear ghee on one side of the chapatii. Fold it in half, smear some more ghee and fold in half again. Now roll out into a triangular shape. Cook on a hot tava but do not use ghee at all at this stage. Place on a fire and bake both sides like a phulka, till it puffs up.

Serves : 4-6

KHAMEERI PURI
(Deep-fried, Flavoured Yeast Bread)

250 gm wheat flour	300 gm ghee
250 gm flour	4 tblsp sugar
$1/2$ tsp salt	$1/2$ cup milk (approx)
1 tblsp sonf (powdered)	2 tblsp curd
2 tblsp khameer	1 tsp khus-khus
(preferably jalebi	a pinch of zafran
khameer)	

Mix together the wheat flour, flour and salt, and sieve. Add sonf; khameer and two tablespoons of ghee. In a large bowl (as the dough swells up with the yeast overnight), mix sugar into the milk. Now put in the wheat flour/flour mixture, knead with a little warm water and the sweetened milk. Continue the process for at least fifteen minutes till the dough becomes soft. Keep it covered in a vessel in a warm place for about eight to ten hours so that the mixture rises.

Now take out enough dough to make puris, about three-inch each in diameter. (Either press them with your fingers on the rolling board or roll the dough lightly with a roller, using a little oil.) In a separate vessel, mix whipped curd with a little sugar, khus-khus and zafran. Smear this mixture lightly on one side of each puri only. Deep fry in hot ghee till the puris are golden brown.

Serve with any vegetable bhujia, minced meat or sweetened curd, flavoured with zafran and garnished with kishmish.

Note : To make khameer at home, follow this method: Take a cup of flour, half a teaspoon of sugar, one spoon of salt and a quarter cup of curd. Mix together, make into a thin batter and keep it in a warm place. It will ferment overnight and turn into khameer.

To make Khameeri Puri in the morning, begin the kneading process the previous evening and leave the mixture overnight. If the dough is too hard it will not rise properly.

Serves : 10-12

LUCHAI PURI
(Quick-fried Flour Bread)

400 gm ghee or   **1 kg maida**
    vegetable oil

Put the flour in a large bowl, make a hole in the centre and gradually pour in two cups of water. Mix and knead well to form a soft dough, adding more water if necessary. Make twelve to sixteen balls of equal size and roll each one into a thin chapatti (with a little dry flour) about eight to nine inches in diameter.

Heat the ghee in a karhai and put in the chapattis, one at a time, and deep fry quickly. (An old saying is: "Dala, Palta, Nikala', which is: put in, turn over and remove, all within a minute or so. It must never be fried longer.) Use a flat, perforated ladle for handling the puris. Keep in a covered vessel.

Note : Luchai Puri is often eaten with powdered sugar (boora) as a sweet dish, and is usually made on festive occasions.

Serves : 12-16

SHEERMAL
(Flavoured Sweet Bread)

1 kg flour	25 gm kishmish
$1/2$ tsp salt	200 gm khoya
125 gm sugar	2 tblsp khameer
2 cups milk	a pinch of zafran
1 tblsp sonf (slightly crushed)	1 tsp khus-khus

Mix the salt with the flour, and sieve. Add sugar to the milk and set aside. In a large pan, put in the flour and add sonf and kishmish.

Now mix the khoya and flour together and rub them well with your fingers. When this is done, put the mixture into a bowl, and make a hole in the centre. Pour the sweetened milk and yeast into the depression, mix the flour gradually and knead well for about fifteen minutes. If the dough feels stiff, add a little lukewarm water and knead again. Cover with a damp cloth and keep in a warm place till the dough rises. (This preparation should preferably be made at night, so that by the next morning the dough has risen satisfactorily.)

Take eight circular or oval baking tins, at least nine inches in diameter and grease them with a little cooking oil. Divide the dough into eight equal balls and flatten each ball in the greased tins. Smear the surface with the ground zafran and khus-khus. This should be done a few hours before baking.

Put the tins into a moderately hot oven and bake for about fifteen minutes or till the surface turns light brown.

Serves : 20-25

SWEETS

FIRNI
(Creamy Rice Pudding)

1 litre milk	a pinch of zafran
100 gm khoya (optional)	1 tsp keora water
75 gm rice flour	300 gm sugar
10 pistas	5 or 6 choti elaichis
10 badams (shelled,	(crushed)
soaked and skinned)	4 silver leaves

Put the milk in a karhai and place on a slow fire. Dissolve the khoya and the rice flour by using half a cup of milk from the karhai. Set aside. Finely shred the pistas and badam. Grind the zafran in keora water and set aside. Add the dissolved khoya and rice flour to the milk gradually and keep stirring with a spatula so that it does not adhere to the bottom and burn. As the milk becomes thick enough to coat the back of the spatula put in sugar and remove the vessel from the fire. As it cools, mix in the crushed choti elaichi and keora water.

Note : Firni is usually served cold. Keep it in a cool place or a refrigerator for some hours before serving. Earthen cups give Firni a special flavour. Use silver leaves and shredded nuts to decorate as in the recipe for Siwain ki Kheer. Take care to use fresh khoya; stale khoya may curdle the milk.

Serves : 8

KHEER
(Rich Rice Pudding)

1 litre milk	a pinch of zafran
100 gm khoya (optional)	1 tsp keora water
75 gm rice (soaked)	300 gm sugar
10 pistas	5 to 6 choti elaichis
10 badams (shelled,	(crushed)
soaked and skinned)	4 silver leaves

The process is almost the same as for Firni, except that the rice added to the milk should be stirred constantly with a ladle, so that the mixture does not stick to the bottom, and the milk, rice and other ingredients are blended to a thick consistency. Add sugar and remove vessel from the fire. Decorate and serve like Firni.

Note : The difference between Kheer and Firni is that in the former soaked whole rice is used whereas in the latter, rice flour or soaked ground rice is used.

Serves : 8

SIWAIN KI KHEER
(Vermicelli Pudding with Dry Fruits)

125 gm ghee or	4 silver leaves
vegetable oil	15 gm pista and badam
60 gm siwain (vermicelli)	(shelled)
1 litre milk	a pinch of zafran
250 gm sugar	1 tsp keora water

In a vessel (preferably an iron karhai) put in the ghee and fry the siwain, in batches till it acquires a reddish tinge. Set aside. (The left-over ghee may be utilized for another dish.)

Put milk in the vessel and bring it to a boil. When it is about to thicken, put in the fried siwain. Allow to simmer for a few minutes till the siwain is soft and the milk has thickened. Add sugar and remove the vessel from the fire.

Note : Siwain ki Kheer is usually served cold in earthen cups (sakore), which not only provide a delightful flavour of their own, but absorb the extra moisture in the kheer. The top of the kheer is covered with silver leaf and shredded pistas and badam are sprinkled over it. Zafran, ground in keora water, is also sprinkled over.

Serves : 8-10

SIWAIN
(Rich Flavoured Vermicelli)

$\frac{1}{2}$ kg siwain (white)
$\frac{1}{2}$ kg ghee
5 or 6 choti elaichis
   (crushed)
a pinch of zafran
   (ground finely)

750 gm sugar
1 tsp keora water
25 gm kishmish
10 gm badam (shelled)
$\frac{1}{2}$ cup milk
2 silver leaves

Fry the siwain in small batches in ghee, in a karhai, till they acquire a golden-brown colour. Strain and set aside. In a wide-bottomed vessel, put in the siwain and add water to just about cover it. Do not pour more water than directed. Cook on a slow fire till the siwain swells and the water evaporates. Add sugar and mix gently. Stir it carefully so that the sugar mixes with the siwain. Then add the elaichi, zafran, keora water, kishmish and badam.

Stir gently again till the ingredients are well mixed. For

best results, place the vessel on a charcoal fire, cover with a lid and place some live charcoals on top. Leave it thus till the water released by the sugar is completely absorbed by the siwain. Add milk, a little at a time, and cover again. Decorate with silver leaves, and serve hot.

Serves : 6-8

KHUBANI
(Dried Apricots in Syrup)

20 dried apricots
150 gm sugar
6 choti elaichis
a pinch of zafran
1 tsp keora water

250 gm chaman
125 gm ghee or
   vegetable oil
maida or corn floor

Soak the dry apricots, overnight, in water. Next morning, drain the water and set the apricots aside. Prepare a syrup with the sugar, of a slightly thick consistency. Add the apricots while the syrup is hot and allow to simmer on a slow fire for ten minutes. Shell the elaichi, pound lightly, and add to the apricots. Grind the zafran in keora water and put it in as well. Serve hot.

Chaman Khubani : Mash the chaman with the palm of your hand till it becomes a soft homogenous mass. Add one-sixteenth of its weight of cornflour or maida and mix well again.

Form balls of one-inch diameter and press them slightly flat. Fry in hot ghee till they turn reddish brown and put them into the hot syrup, just as you would the khubani. (Do not use a ladle too often or it will break the khubanis.)

Serves : 6-8

MEETHA CHAVAL—ZARDA / MACHAMA
(Saffron Rice Pudding)

$^1/_2$ kg rice
100 gm ghee
25 gm kishmish
25 gm badam (shelled,
   soaked and skinned)
4 pieces of laung
750 gm sugar

a pinch of zafran
1 tsp keora water
5 or 6 choti elaichis
   (crushed)
1 cup milk
2 silver leaves
edible yellow colourant

Soak the rice for an hour, drain and set aside. Heat the ghee and when hot, put in the kishmish and badam. When the kishmish swell, strain and set aside. Put in the laung in the remaining ghee. After a few seconds, add the soaked rice and fry for a few minutes. Pour water (one and a quarter times the weight of the soaked

rice) and allow to boil. When the rice has absorbed the water (but is still not completely cooked) add the sugar. Mix with the handle of a ladle. Grind the zafran in keora water and crush the elaichi seeds. Add, and mix them into the rice along with badam and kishmish.

Place the vessel on a slow fire and cover. (For best results, place the vessel on a charcoal fire with a few live coals on the lid.) Add milk and keep the vessel on the fire for another ten minutes. To acquire a darker shade of golden yellow, mix in a pinch of edible yellow colourant. Decorate with silver leaves. Serve hot.

Serves : 4-6

PANJEERI
(Rich Traditional Pandit Delicacy)

300 gms chhuaara (cut)	125 gm dry coconut
125 gm makkhana	(shredded and cut)
300 gm ghee	125 gm badam (shelled
65 gm khus-khus	and cut into halves)
125 gm kharbuze ke beej	1 tsp keora water
a large pinch of zafran	2 tsp haldi
(ground)	$1^1/_2$ kg sugar

Cut the chhuaaras into pieces, a quarter of an inch thick, soak overnight in enough water to cover the pieces. Boil next morning, till they absorb an adequate amount of water and become soft. Strain and save the excess water in another vessel. Cut the makkhanas into two and fry them quickly in the ghee till they become crisp. Remove and set aside. Put the khus-khus in the ghee and fry it quickly.

In a karhai, roast the kharbuze ke beej till they swell

and start popping. Do not allow them to scorch or turn brown. Set aside.

In a large bhagona, put in all the ingredients, including the ghee, but not the sugar. Add water (which had been kept aside) one-inch above the level of the ingredients and boil till the makkhane become soft. Add the sugar and allow to simmer till it forms a thick syrup. Panjeeri is served hot.

Note : To test the consistency of the syrup, dip the tip of your forefinger into the liquid. If the consistency is correct, on pressing your finger and thumb together; then separating them, the syrup will appear sticky and form at least three or four threads.

Serves : 40

SUJI OR BESAN KA HALWA
(Semolina or Gram Flour Halwa)

250 gm ghee or vegetable oil	1 tsp chironji
	1 tsp keora water
250 gm semolina or gram flour	25 gm kishmish
	1 silver leaf
250 gm sugar	15 gm badam (shelled)
2 cups water	or kaju (optional)
5 choti elaichis (crushed)	15 gm pista (optional)

In a karhai or frying pan, put in the ghee, add semolina or gram flour and fry, stirring constantly till it becomes light brown. Add sugar and water. Allow to simmer for a few minutes, stirring continuously to avoid burning at the bottom. When dry, remove from fire. Crush elaichi seeds, and add them, with the chironji, keora water and kishmish, to the halwa.

If using semolina, it should swell to almost double its volume after adding water. Add more water, if necessary. When the gram flour gives out a roasted flavour, sugar and water should be added. When the halwa is ready, remove it from the fire, turn it into a dish and spread the silver leaf over it. Dress it with shredded badam or kaju and pistas. Serve hot.

Serves : 6-8

CHANE KI DAL KA HALWA
(Flavoured Yellow Lentils Halwa)

250 gm chane ki dal
250 gm ghee or
    vegetable oil
250 gm sugar
5 choti elaichis (ground)
1 tsp chironji

15 gm badam (shelled,
    soaked, skinned and
    shredded)
25 gm kishmish
a drop of keora essence
1 silver leaf

Soak dal in water for two or three hours, drain and grind coarsely. Set aside.

Heat the ghee in any vessel or frying pan, and when hot put in the ground dal. Stir continuously till it is lightly fried. Add sugar and a cup of water. Stir again. Now add the ground elaichi, chironji, a few shredded badams and kishmish. When the water is absorbed and ghee appears on the surface, add a drop of keora essence and mix. Turn the halwa on to a plate, dress with the silver leaf, and decorate with the remaining badam. Serve hot.

Serves : 6-8

GAJAR KA HALWA
(Carrot Halwa)

1 kg gajar (medium size)	10 choti elaichis
1 litre milk	(shelled)
150 gm ghee	25 gm kishmish
50 gm khoya	15 gm badam (shelled)
150 gm sugar	or kaju
a drop of keora essence	1 silver leaf

Wash and finely grate the gajar. Put in the grated gajar and milk in a karhai, add a cup of water and boil till the gajar becomes soft. Allow the water to evaporate so that the gajar is dry, but take care that it does not burn at the bottom.

In another vessel, heat the ghee and when hot, add gajar and khoya and fry till the moisture evaporates. Add sugar, a drop of keora essence, and keep stirring till ghee appears on the surface. Put in the elaichi, kishmish and half the shredded badam or kaju. Spread the halwa on a plate, apply silver leaf and decorate with the remaining badam or kaju. Serve hot.

Serves : 6-8

ROATH
(Kashmiri Snack)

1 kg wheat flour	250 gm sugar
200 gm ghee (for	$\frac{1}{2}$ tsp khus-khus
mixing)	500 gm ghee (for frying)

Mix 200 gm of ghee in with the flour. Rub it in well. Mix the sugar with one and a half cup of water in a bowl.

When the sugar has dissolved, add it to the flour. Knead well and make a stiff dough. Add more water, if necessary.

Make eight balls of equal size with the dough and roll them into half-inch thick rounds, about eight to nine inches in diameter. Pierce them with a fork all over, sprinkle a little khus-khus on top and press it in lightly. Fry in medium-hot ghee till they are reddish brown.

Note : Roaths are usually prepared at the time of the Kashmiri festival, Pun. After rolling the roath, it is usually decorated by marking it with designs and pinching the edges to form scallops.

Makes : 8 pieces

MURABBA
(Preserve)

1 kg of mango, apple,
   ash gourd, carrot or
   guava
2 or 3 drops of keora
   essence

1¹/₂ kg sugar
lime water slaked (1 tsp
   of lime disintegrated
   in half a bucket
   of water)

Peel, wash and cut large, lengthwise sections of whichever fruit or vegetable your choose. Prick the cut pieces all over with a fork, and soak them in lime water for several hours. This makes them crisp. Then wash again in clean water and boil till they are half tender.

In a separate vessel, make a syrup by boiling the sugar in four cups of water. Put in the boiled fruit or vegetable and boil again for half an hour. Remove from fire, cover and allow fruit to remain in the syrup for one whole night. Next morning, boil again till the syrup thickens to the desired consistency (three to four threads). Add keora essence. When the murabba is cool, store in sterilized bottles.

Note : Test the consistency of the syrup by dipping the tips of your thumb and forefinger into it. On separating your thumb and forefinger, two threads will form.

PICKLES AND CHUTNEYS

PICKLES AND CHUTNEYS

PANI KA ACHAAR
(Water-based Vegetable Pickle)

1 kg of potatoes, turnips, cauliflower, beans, carrots or all mixed together	¼ tsp hing
	1 tsp lal mirch powder
	2 tblsp mustard seed (rai ground coarsely)
2 tsp salt	2 tblsp mustard oil
1½ tsp haldi	1 inch piece gur

Peel and cut the potatoes into halves. Cut the turnips into half-inch thick slices, and the beans into halves. Break up the cauliflower into small florets. Scrape the carrots and slit it length-wise.

Now boil all the vegetables in water till half done. Drain and set aside. In either a wide-mouthed earthen vessel or an aluminium bhagona, mix the boiled vegetables with the masalas and mustard oil. Cover and keep in the sun for two days.

Next, pour enough boiling water to cover the vegetables, and add the gur. Leave the vessel in the sun and shake it twice a day. After four to five days, the liquid begins to turn sour and the pickle is ready.

Note : As the pickles are consumed, fresh boiled vegetables may be added, they are ready to eat within a day. This pickle can also be made without adding boiled water, in which case it is a dry pickle.

TEL KA ACHAAR
(Oil-based Mango / Lemon Pickle)

Ingredients for the first method

25 raw mangoes (medium sized)	salt, equalling the weight of all the mango seeds
2 tsp sonf	1 tblsp lal mirch powder
3 tsp methi dana	3 tsp haldi
3 tblsp rai	2 tsp kalonji
1/2 tsp hing	1 kg mustard oil

Either peel the mangoes or leave them in their skins. Wash, wipe and cut them in fours or eights. Roast the sonf and methi dana lightly and grind them with the rai. Mix the remaining masalas with the pieces of mango, with a little mustard oil, and store in a jar. Tie a piece of linen to the mouth of the jar. Cover and keep it in the sun for three to four days. Now remove the cloth and add the rest of the mustard oil which should stand an inch above the surface of the mangoes. The pickle will be soft and ready in a month.

Ingredients for the second method

25 raw mangoes (medium sized)	2 tsp sonf
2 tsp kalonji	2 tblsp dhania
1 tblsp lal mirch powder	3 tsp haldi
salt, equalling the weight of all the mango seeds	1/2 tsp hing
2 tsp methi dana	150 gm garlic (coarsely ground)
	500 gm mustard oil

Do not peel the mangoes. Mix the sliced pieces with salt, put them in a jar and leave it in the sun for three days. Drain out all the water released by the mangoes and spread them on a piece of cloth to dry. Roast all the masalas, including kalonji, (but no salt) lal mirch, haldi, hing and garlic, and grind to a powder. Mix in everything with the pieces of mango and put them in a jar. Pour the mustard oil into the mixture and leave the jar in the sun for three to four days. Well preserved, this pickle can last for over a year.

Note : Never dip wet spoons or hands into the pickle containers.

TAMATAR KI CHUTNEY
(Tomato Chutney)

4 kg ripe red tomatoes	50 gm ginger (ground)
50 gm garlic (ground)	300 gm gur
salt and lal mirch powder to taste	1 cup malt or pure vinegar

Steam the tomatoes, skin, and remove the pulp. Put this in a vessel and allow to simmer till it thickens. Add the ground garlic, masala and gur. Stir constantly as the gur dissolves. As the chutney thickens, add the vinegar and allow to simmer till you obtain a fairly thick consistency. Strain through a wire sieve, or soup strainer using a wooden spoon to remove any lumps or skin.

BHUNE AAM KI CHUTNEY
(Roasted Mango Chutney)

25 raw mangoes (3 inch
  size)
1 tsp kalonji
1 tsp zeera
$\frac{1}{2}$ tsp hing
lal mirch powder to taste
2 to 3 cups vinegar
  (pure)
25 gm kishmish

25 gm chhuaara (cut
  into small cubes)
1 inch piece ginger
  (shredded finely)
2 cloves garlic (shelled
  and ground; optional)
500 gm sugar or gur
salt to taste

Have the mango roasted in hot sand or wash and put them in the containers of a pressure cooker, and cook for five minutes or till they are soft. Remove. When cool squeeze out the pulp from each mango, with your hands, into an enamel or aluminium vessel. Throw away the skin and seed. Mix all the ingredients and the vinegar well. Add more vinegar if the chutney is too thick. (Use a wooden spoon for this operation). Taste a little and add sugar or salt, whichever is necessary, according to taste. Put it in tightly covered jars and place in the sun for a few days.

Note : No water should be used at any stage in this chutney or it will ferment.

TEA AND SNACKS

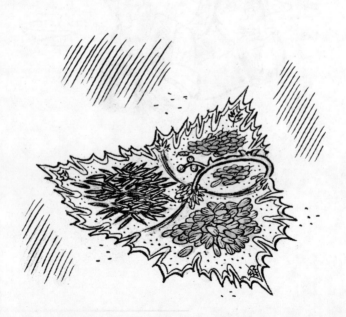

KASSAR
(Dry, Flavoured Semolina—Wheat Flour Mixture)

100 gm ghee
25 gm makkhana (cut
   into halves)
750 gm wheat flour
250 gm semolina
25 gm chironji

25 gm kishmish
25 gm badam (shelled
   and cut into halves)
50 gm dry coconut
   (shredded)
250 gm sugar

Heat ghee in a karhai, and when hot, fry the makkhanas till they turn light brown. Strain and set aside. Put the wheat flour and semolina in the ghee and, using a spatula continuously, fry the mixture till it becomes light brown and emits a roasted flavour. Do not allow it to burn at the bottom. Next, mix in the fried makkhanas, chironji, kishmish, badam and the shredded coconut, and remove the vessel from the fire. Add sugar and mix well. When the Kassar cools, store it in an airtight container.

Note : Kassar may also be prepared with semolina only. It is usually made at the time of a puja in Kashmiri Pandit homes. It is also a favourite snack with children.

KHAJOOR
(Sweet Fried Biscuits)

200 gm ghee (for mixing)
1 kg flour

50 gm sugar
500 gm ghee (for frying)

Mix ghee with the flour and rub well with the palms of your hands. Add sugar and rub again.

In a bowl, put in the mixed flour and enough water to

make a stiff dough. Set aside for two hours. Then form the dough into two-inch balls and flatten them with your palms to an oval shape, about three-quarters of an inch long and half an inch thick. Prick all over with a fork.

Khajoors usually have a design on either side. This can easily be done by pressing each side against an inverted bamboo basket, or pressing them with an inverted fork.

In a karhai, put in 500 gms of ghee and when hot, fry the khajoors, three or four at a time, turning them over every few minutes till they are reddish brown.

Note : Do not use high heat. This tends to burn the khajoor on the outside, leaving the inside undone. Use medium heat, too low a heat will make them crumble.

SOHAL
(Salty Crisp Snack)

700 gm ghee or vegetable oil (200 gm for mixing, 500 gm for frying)	**1 kg flour**
	3 tsp salt
	1 tsp ajwain

Sieve the flour, add salt and ajwain, and mix well. Add 200 gm of the ghee to the flour and rub it well with your hands till it is thoroughly mixed. Use a little water to make it into a stiff dough. Now form eight to ten balls from the dough and roll each on a board till they are the size of chappatis, and one-eighth of an inch thick.

Make incisions on them with a knife, an inch apart. Fry in medium-hot ghee till they are golden in colour. Drain on a clean sheet of paper or in a small bamboo basket.

Note : Do not fry in very hot ghee or the Sohal will turn brown on the outside and remain underdone in the centre. Use medium heat.

TAKTAKI
(Spicy Thick Bread)

250 gm whole wheat flour	$1/2$ tsp zeera
$1/2$ tsp salt	a pinch of hing
1 tsp peppercorns	a pinch of ajwain
(crushed)	$1/2$ cup milk
$1/2$ tsp sonf	

Mix the masala with the wheat flour, pour in the milk and knead to form a stiff dough. Should the dough become too stiff use a little water to soften. Now scoop out small lumps of dough and roll them on a rolling board to make thick chappatis, about three to four inches in diameter and a quarter of an inch thick.

Pierce on one side with a fork and bake on a hot tava till both sides become brown, turning the Taktaki frequently. Cook in medium heat.

NAMAK PARE
(Salty Strips)

½ kg flour or whole
   wheat flour or both
   equally mixed
1 tsp salt

15 peppercorns (crushed)
½ tsp ajwain
250 gm ghee (for frying)
100 gm ghee (for mixing)

Prepare the dough as for Taktaki, using the above ingredients. Roll the dough out on a rolling board to a quarter of an inch thickness. Cut strips half an inch wide and cut again crosswise, so that each piece is about three-quarters of an inch long (or smaller or bigger, as you prefer). Deep fry in hot ghee till they turn golden brown. Cook on medium heat.

SHAKKAR PARE
(Sweet Strips)

½ kg flour or whole
   wheat flour or both,
   equally mixed
150 gm sugar

15 peppercorns (crushed;
   optional)
250 gm ghee (for frying)
100 gm ghee (for mixing)

These are usually cut smaller in size. The rest of the process is the same as for Namak Pare.

KASHMIRI TEA

Though most Kashmiri Pandit families settled in the plains drink only the well-known brands of tea in the usual western style, there are some homes where green tea is still brewed in a samovar, a jug-like vessel with a funnel in the middle. The funnel has a grill at the bottom so the live charcoal placed in it does not fall out.

KEHWA
(Kashmiri Green Tea)

4 cups water
1 tsp fresh green tea
2 choti elaichis
   (powdered)

a pinch of dalchini
   (powdered)
3 or 4 badams (shredded)
sugar to taste

Pour the water into a vessel, add tea leaves and allow it to boil. As it boils, add sugar to taste. Put in the elaichi, dalchini and shredded badam and cover. The tea is now ready to drink.

SAMOVAR TEA

6 cups water
3 cups milk
10 tsp sugar
1/2 inch piece dalchini
a pinch of sodium
   bicarbonate

4 choti elaichis
2 tsp fresh green tea
   or
2 tsp fresh Ladakh (loose
   tea or cubes)

Put water, milk, sugar and all the ingredients except the sodium bicarbonate into the outer chamber of the samovar. Now put in five or six large live charcoals in the funnel and allow the tea to brew for at least an hour. Then add the sodium bicarbonate (this enhances the colour of the tea which becomes a pinkish red). The tea flows out through a small tap fitted to the bottom of the samovar.

If you do not have a samovar, you can brew this tea in a bhagona.

SHEER CHA
(Salty Cream Tea)

6 cups water
1 tsp green tea
a pinch of sodium
   bicarbonate

salt to taste
1 1/2 cups milk
1 tblsp cream (if desired)

Put a cup of water in a vessel, add the tea leaves and
the sodium bicarbonate and boil, till only five or six
teaspoons of liquid remain. Now add another cup of
water and boil till only a little is left. Next, add four cups
of water and salt to taste. After this has boiled for a few
minutes, the colour of the tea will become pink. Pour in
the milk. Do not cover the tea while it is cooking. When
it has boiled for some time, take it off the fire. When
serving, add cream.

NUN CHA
(Salty Tea)

This has the same ingredients and method as Sheer
Cha, but no milk or cream is used.

GLOSSARY

Hindustani	English
Aam	Mango
Adrak	Ginger
Ajwain	Thymol (an aromatic seed)
Alu	Potato
Alu Bukhara	Dried Plums
Amchur	Dried green mango powder
Arvi	Species of yam
Atta	Whole wheat flour
Badam	Almonds
Baigan	Brinjal
Bajra	Millet
Banda	Yam
Bandh Gobhi / Karmakalla	Cabbage
Bari Elaichi	Cardamom
Batian	Mixed spice cakes (Kashmiri)
Bel	Wood apple
Belan	Rolling pin
Besan	Gram flour
Bhagona	Wide-mouthed vessel
Bheja	Brain
Bhindi	Okra
Chakla	Rolling board
Chhalni	Sieve
Chana	Bengal gram
Chashni	Syrup
Chaval	Rice
Chaval ka Atta	Rice flour
Chaman / Paneer / Chhena	Cottage cheese
Chhuaara	Dried dates
Chilka	Outer covering of pulses
Chironji	Small sapid nut
Choti Elaichi	Cardamom
Chukandar	Beetroot
Chumta	Tongs

Dahi	Curd/yoghurt
Dal	Lentils/pulses
Dalchini	Cinnamon
Daniwal / Dhania	Coriander
Dast	Foreleg of mutton
Degchi	Vessel
Dhuli	Washed
Gajar	Carrot
Ganth Gobhi	Knol Khol
Garam masala	Pungent spices
Gehun ka Atta	Wheat flour
Ghee	Clarified butter
Gosht	Meat
Guchchi	Mushrooms (dried)
Gulab jal	Rose water
Gur	Jaggery
Gurde	Kidneys
Haldi	Turmeric
Hara dhania	Green coriander
Hari mirch	Green chillies
Hathichak	Artichoke
Hing	Asafoetida
Imli	Tamarind
Jaiphal	Nutmeg
Jalebi khameer	Yeast used to prepare jalebis
Jau	Barley
Javitri	Mace
Jharna	Perforated ladle
Kabuli chana	Chick peas
Kachnar	Edible flower of the Bauhinia tree
Kaddu	Pumpkin
Kali mirch	Black pepper
Kaju	Cashewnut
Kakri/Kheera	Cucumber

Kaleji	Liver
Kalonji	Onion seeds
Kapure	Testes
Karamkalla	Cabbage
Karchi	Ladle
Karela	Bitter gourd
Kathal	Jackfruit
Katori	Small metal bowl
Kela	Banana
Keora	The fragrant flower Pandanus
Khameer	Yeast
Kharbuze ke beej	Melon seeds (dried and peeled)
Khatta	Sour
Kheema	Minced meat
Khoya	Thickened milk
Khus-khus	Poppy seeds
Kishmish	Raisins
Lal mirch	Red chillies
Lauki	Bottle gourd
Lehsun	Garlic
Lobhia	String beans
Laung/Lavang	Cloves
Machhli	Fish
Maida	Refined white flour
Makkhane	Lotus seeds
Masoor	Lentil (red)
Matar	Peas
Meetha	Sweet
Methi	Fenugreek
Methi dana	Fenugreek seeds
Mirch	Chillies
Misri	Crystallized sugar
Mowal	Extract of cockscomb flowers
Muli	Radish
Murgh	Chicken
Nadru	Lotus root

Narial	Coconut
Nashpati	Pear
Nimbu/Neebu	Lime/lemon
Palak	Spinach
Paneer	Cottage cheese
Papita	Papaya
Parwal	Variety of gherkin
Patua	Sorrel
Paye	Trotters
Petha	Ash gourd (white pumpkin)
Phepra	Lungs
Phool Gobhi	Cauliflower
Pista	Pistachio
Pudina	Mint
Rai	Mustard seed
Ran	Hing leg of mutton
Ras	Gravy
Rasdaar	With gravy
Ratalu	Yam
Razmah	Kidney beans
Sabudana	Sago
Saag	Leafy vegetable
Sabut	Whole
Salad	Lettuce
Santra	Orange
Seb	Apple
Sehjan	Drumsticks
Sem	Broad beans
Shah zeera	Black cumin seeds
Shakkar	Sugar
Shakarkandi	Sweet potato
Shaljam	Turnip
Shehad	Honey
Sirka	Vinegar
Siwain	Vermicelli
Sonf	Aniseed
Sonth	Dried ginger

Succh bari	Mixed spice cakes (Kashmiri)
Suji	Semolina (wheatmeal)
Tava	Iron plate (griddle)
Tejpatta	Bay leaf
Thali	Flat metal plate with upturned rim
Til	Sesame seeds
Tinda	Variety of gourd
Trami	Large metal plate
Turai	Snake gourd
Urad	Black gram
Varakh	Silver leaf
Yakhni	Stock
Zafran	Saffron
Zaminkand	Yam
Zeera	Cumin seeds

INDEX

OF RECIPES

DAL (LENTILS)

DUMS

EGGS

KABABS

MACHHLI (FISH)

MURGH (CHICKEN)

MUTTON

PICKLES AND CHUTNEYS

SNACKS

SAFFRON
FLOWERS